THIS DAY
Wendell Berry

This Day

Sabbath Poems
Collected and New
1979–2013

Wendell Berry

COUNTERPOINT

BERKELEY

Sabbath poems from 1979–1997 originally appeared in *A Timbered Choir*;
1998–2004 in *Given*; 2005–2008 in *Leavings*, all published by Counterpoint.

Author and publisher thank the editors of the following magazines for their
hospitality to some of these poems that have not previously been published
in a book: *Threepenny Review, Sewanee Review, Hudson Review, Terrain,
The Progressive, Temenos Academy Review.*

Library of Congress Cataloging-in-Publication is available.
ISBN 978-1-61902-436-6

Cover design by Gerilyn Attebery
Interior design by David Bullen

COUNTERPOINT
2560 Ninth Street, Suite 318
Berkeley, CA 94710
www.counterpointpress.com

Printed in the United States of America

12

To Donald Hall
and
In Memory of Kathleen Raine

Contents

Preface: *A Timbered Choir*: Sabbath Poems 1979–1997   xix
This Day: An Introduction   xxi

Preface: From Sabbaths 2013
I   *This is a poet of the river lands*   3
II   *Times will come as they must*   4

1979

I   *I go among trees and sit still*   7
II   *Another Sunday morning comes*   8
III   *To sit and look at light-filled leaves*   10
IV   *The bell calls in the town*   11
V   *How many have relinquished*   14
VI   *What stood will stand, though all be fallen*   15
VII   *What if, in the high, restful sanctuary*   16
VIII   *I go from the woods into the cleared field*   18
IX   *Enclosing the field within bounds*   19
X   *Whatever is foreseen in joy*   20
XI   *To long for what can be fulfilled in time*   21
XII   *To long for what eternity fulfills*   23

1980

I   *What hard travail God does in death*   25
II   *The eager dog lies strange and still*   26
III   *Great deathly powers have passed*   27
IV   *The frog with lichened back and golden thigh*   28
V   *Six days of work are spent*   29
VI   *The intellect so ravenous to know*   30

1981

I   *Here where the world is being made*   33

1982

I   *Dream ended, I went out, awake*   35
II   *Here where the dark-sourced stream brims up*   36
III   *The pasture, bleached and cold two weeks ago*   37
IV   *Thrush song, stream song, holy love*   38
V   *A child unborn, the coming year*   39
VI   *We have walked so many times, my boy*   40
VII   *The clearing rests in song and shade*   44
VIII   *Our household for the time made right*   45
IX   *Hail to the forest born again*   46
X   *The dark around us, come*   47

1983

I   *In a crease of the hill*   49
II   *The year relents, and free*   50
III   *Now though the season warms*   52
IV   *Who makes a clearing makes a work of art*   53

1984

I   *Over the river in loud flood*   55
II   *A tired man leaves his labor, felt*   56
III   *The crop must drink; we move the pipe*   59
IV   *The summer ends, and it is time*   60
V   *Estranged by distance, he relearns*   61

1985

I   *Not again in this flesh will I see*   63
II   *A gracious Sabbath stood here while they stood*   64

III	*Awaked from the persistent dream*	65
IV	*The fume and shock and uproar*	66
V	*How long does it take to make the woods*	67
VI	*Life forgives its depredations*	68
VII	*The winter wren is back, quick*	69

1986

| I | *Slowly, slowly, they return* | 71 |

1987

I	*Coming to the woods' edge*	73
II	*I climb up through the thicket*	75
III	*And now the lowland grove is down, the trees*	77
IV	*May what I've written here*	78
V	*And now the remnant groves grow bright with praise*	79
VI	*Remembering that it happened once*	80

1988

I	*Now I have reached the age*	81
II	*It is the destruction of the world*	82
III	*Another year has returned us*	83
IV	*The world of machines is running*	84
V	*Always in the distance*	85

1989

I	*In early morning we awaken from*	87
II	*The old oak wears new leaves*	88
III	*I walked the deserted prospect of the modern mind* [Santa Clara Valley]	89
IV	*Now Loyce Flood is dead*	91
V	*He thought to keep himself from Hell*	92
VI	*One morning out of time*	93

VII	*Here by the road where people are carried, with*	94
VIII	*The sky bright after summer-ending rain*	95
IX	*One day I walked imagining*	96

1990

I	*The two, man and boy, wait*	97
II	*To give mind to machines, they are calling it*	99
III	*After the slavery of the body, dumbfoundment*	100
IV	*I walk in openings*	101
V	*The body in the invisible*	103
VI	*Cut off in front of the line*	104

1991

I	*The year begins with war*	105
II	*The ewes crowd to the mangers*	107
III	*Now with its thunder spring*	108
IV	*The team rests in shade at the edge*	109
V	*The seed is in the ground*	110
VI	*Seventeen more years, and they are here* [The Locusts]	111
VII	*Where the great trees were felled*	112
VIII	*What do the tall trees say*	113
IX	*Go by the narrow road* [The Farm]	114
X	*Loving you has taught me the infinite*	127

1992

I	*The winter world of loss*	129
II	*Lift up the dead leaves*	130
III	*Again we come*	131
IV	*I went away only*	132
V	*I too am not at home*	133
VI	*My sore ran in the night*	134
VII	*Those who give their thought*	135
VIII	*I have again come home*	136
IX	*We have kept to the way we chose* [Thirty-five Years]	138

1993

I	*No, no, there is no going back*	141
II	*When my father was an old man*	142
III	*Now, surely, I am getting old*	143
IV	*Hate has no world*	144
V	*We went in darkness where* [Remembering Evia]	145

1994

I	*I leave the warmth of the stove*	147
II	*Finally will it not be enough*	149
III	*I think of Gloucester, blind, led through the world*	150
IV	*They sit together on the porch, the dark*	151
V	*Raking hay on a rough slope*	152
VI	*A man is lying on a bed*	153
VII	*I would not have been a poet*	154
VIII	*And now this leaf lies brightly on the ground*	155

1995

I	*A man with some authentic worries*	157
II	*The best reward in going to the woods*	158
III	*Worn to brightness, this* [A Brass Bowl]	159
IV	*We live by mercy if we live* [Amish Economy]	160
V	*Now you know the worst*	162
VI	*He had a tall cedar he wanted to cut for posts* [The Old Man Climbs a Tree]	163

1996

I	*Now you have slipped away*	165
II	*On summer evenings we sat in the yard*	166
III	*It is almost spring again*	167
IV	*A long time ago, returning*	168
V	*Some Sunday afternoon, it may be*	169

VI   *A bird the size*   170
VII   *In spring we planted seed*   171
VIII   *Our Christmas tree is*   172

1997

I   *Best of any song*   173
II   *Even while I dreamed I prayed that what I saw*
   was only fear and no foretelling   174
III   *I was wakened from my dream of the ruined*
   world by the sound   176
IV   *"You see," my mother said, and laughed*   177
V   *The lovers know the loveliness*   178
VI   *Now, as a man learning*   179
VII   *There is a day*   181

1998

I   *Whatever happens*   183
II   *This is the time you'd like to stay*   184
III   *Early in the morning, walking*   185
IV   *The woods and pastures are joyous*   186
V   *In a single motion the river comes and goes*   187
VI   *By expenditure of hope*   188
VII   *There is a place you can go*   190
VIII   *Given the solemn river*   191
IX   *What I fear most is despair*   192
X   *Tanya. Now that I am getting old*   193

1999

I   *Can I see the buds that are swelling*   195
II   *I dream of a quiet man*   196
III   *The spring woods hastening now*   197
IV   *What a consolation it is, after*   198
V   *In Heaven the starry saints will wipe away*   199

VI   We travelers, walking to the sun, can't see   200
VII   Again I resume the long   201
VIII   The difference is a polished   202
IX   The incarnate Word is with us   203

2000

I   In the world forever one   205
II   When we convene again   206
III   As timely as a river   207
IV   The house is cold at dawn   208
V   I know for a while again   209
VI   Alone, afoot, in moonless night   210
VII   Some had derided him   211
VIII   We hear way off approaching sounds   212
IX   I've come down from the sky   213
X   We follow the dead to their graves   215

2001

I   He wakes in darkness. All around   217
II   Surely it will be for this: the redbud   218
III   Ask the world to reveal its quietude   219
IV   A mind that has confronted ruin for years   220
V   The wind of the fall is here   221
VI   The question before me, now that I   222

2002

I   Late winter cold   223
II   After a mild winter   224
III   We come at last to the dark   226
IV   The Acadian flycatcher, not   227
V   The cherries turn ripe, ripe   228
VI   Is this the river of life   229
VII   The flocking blackbirds fly across   232

VIII   *Every afternoon the old turtle*   233
IX   *All yesterday afternoon I sat*   234
X   *Teach me work that honors Thy work*   235

2003

I   *The woods is white with snow*   237
II   *The kindly faithful light returns*   238
III   *Come to the window, look out, and see* [Look Out]   239
IV   *The little stream sings*   241
V   *The politics of illusion, of death's money*   242
VI   *The yellow-throated warbler, the highest remotest voice*   243
VII   *This, then, is to be the way? Freedom's candle will be*   244
VIII   *All that patriotism requires, and all that it can be*   245
IX   *After the campaign of the killing machines*   246
X   *But do the Lords of War in fact*   247
XI   *It is late November, Thanksgiving*   248

2004

I   *A young man leaving home*   249
II   *They come singly, the little streams*   251
III   *They are fighting again the war to end war*   252
IV   *To think of gathering all*   253
V   *I built a timely room beside the river*   254
VI   *Up in the blown-down woods*   255
VII   *A gracious lady came to us*   256
VIII   *It takes all time to show eternity*   257
IX   *I mistook your white head for a flower*   258
X   *An old man, who has been on many days*   259

2005

I   *I know that I have life*   261
II   *They gather like an ancestry*   262
III   *"Are you back to normal?" asks*   263

IV   We were standing by the road   264
V   Nell's small grave, opening   265
VI   How simple to be dead!—the only   266
VII   I know I am getting old and I say so   267
VIII   I tremble with gratitude   268
IX   Here in the woods near   269
X   Mowing the hillside pasture—where   270
XI   My young grandson rides with me   272
XII   If we have become a people incapable   273
XIII   Eternity is not infinity   274
XIV   God, how I hate the names   275
XV   The painter Harlan Hubbard said   276
XVI   I am hardly an ornithologist   277
XVII   Hardly escaping the limitless machines   280
XVIII   A hawk in flight   281
XIX   Born by our birth   282

                        2006

I   If there are a "chosen few"   283
II   Many I loved as man and boy
        [Old Man Jayber Crow]   284
III   Camp Branch, my native stream
        [The Book of Camp Branch]   285
IV   The times are disgusting enough   290
V   Little stream, Camp Branch, flowing   291
VI   O saints, if I am even eligible for this prayer   292
VII   Before we kill another child   294
VIII   How can we be so superior   295
IX   "That's been an oak tree a long time"   296

                        2007

I   I dream by night the horror   297
II   The nation is a boat   299
III   Yes, though hope is our duty   301

                        XV

IV	In our consciousness of time	302
V	Those who use the world assuming	304
VI	It is hard to have hope. It is harder as you grow old	305
VII	In time a man disappears	307
VIII	Poem, do not raise your voice	308
IX	I go by a field where once	309
X	I love the passing light	310
XI	The sounds of engines leave the air	311
XII	Learn by little the desire for all things	312
XIII	"The past above, the future below	313

2008

I	After the bitter nights	315
II	A man's desire, overwhelming	316
III	Inside its bends, the river	317
IV	A man is walking in a field	318
V	How many of your birthdays	319
VI	For the third time since the first [The Locusts]	320
VII	Having written some pages in favor of Jesus	321
VIII	Hell is timely, for Hell is the thought	322
IX	As if suddenly, little towns	323
X	So many times I've gone away	325
XI	Though he was ill and in pain	326
XII	We forget the land we stand on	327
XIII	By its own logic, greed	328

2009

I	Early in the year by my friend's gift	329
II	We've come again to a garden begun	330
III	After windstorm and ice storm	331
IV	How little I know in my widest	332
V	Tiny elegant birds, a pair, have come	333
VI	Our vow is the plumb line	334
VII	For the apparent disorder	335
VIII	As old men often have said	336

IX	The old know well the world	339
X	Our young Tanya, who bears	340
XI	O Thou who by Thy touch give form	341
XII	At the end of a long time	342

2010

I	When icy fangs hang from the eaves	343
II	Many with whom I mourned the dead	345
III	Where he sat in a room apart	346
IV	Fifty-three years gone	347
V	The red-eyed vireo	348
VI	Let us not condemn the human beings	349
VII	Blesséd be the vireo	351
VIII	If you love it, do not photograph	352
IX	By courtesy of the light	353
X	Anger at humans, my own kind	354
XI	The need comes on me now	355
XII	To those who love one another	356
XIII	O my own small country, battered	357

2011

I	Matisse's Dominique of Vence	359
II	Moonlight, daylight	361
III	Quiet. The river flows soundlessly by	362
IV	At the woods' edge, suddenly	363
V	For years around the spare house	364
VI	The old shepherd comes to another	365
VII	A man who loves the trees	366
VIII	Off in the woods in the quiet	367
IX	I have watched this place	368
X	I saw a hummingbird stand	369
XI	New come, we took fields	370
XII	Do not live for death	372
XIII	Will-lessly the leaves fall	373

2012

I	Now falls upon our hope and work	375
II	Like light beyond "the visible spectrum"	376
III	Though his tenure on the earth	377
IV	It's spring. The birds sing	379
V	The grass doth wither, the flower	380
VI	"Attend to the little ones"	381
VII	Under the sign of the citizen's pistol	382
VIII	Since, despite the stern demands	383
IX	I rest in the one life	384
X	The creek flows full over the rocks	385
XI	There are seasons enough for sorrow	386
XII	Once there was nothing,	387
XIII	The eastern sky at evening	388
XIV	Praise "family values"	389
XV	On a bright day, having slept	391
XVI	There is no spring flower so	392
XVII	After the long weeks	393
XVIII	This is the flood road	394
XIX	This is the age of our absence from the world, even	395
XX	Sit and be quiet. In a while	396
XXI	As a child, the Mad Farmer saw easily	397

❀❁❀❁❀❁❀❁❀❁❀❁❀❁❀❁❀❁❀❁❀❁❀❁❀❁❀❁❀❁❀❁

Preface: *A Timbered Choir*: Sabbath Poems 1979–1997

Over the past four decades, public readings of poetry have attracted a significant audience. With the obvious qualifications, I think this is a good thing. It requires us to be aware that a poem need not be just a fabric of printed words to be laboriously raveled out by students or critics, but is (or can be) written in a speakable and hearable language, the integrity of which begins and ends in the quality of its music. Public readings require us to be aware also that a poem can be a way of saying something of public interest in public: a way of making an argument, of declaring one's allegiance, of taking a stand.

This renewed public life of poetry, however, makes it necessary to say of the poems in this book that they were not conceived or written primarily as statements to be read aloud in public. I have no doubt that they can be so read; sometimes they concern themselves with issues of public importance, and I have tried always to be attentive to the way they sound when spoken aloud. What I am talking about is not necessarily a conflict. But though I am happy to think that poetry may be reclaiming its public life, I am equally happy to insist that poetry also has a private life that is more important to it and more necessary to us.

These poems were written in silence, in solitude, mainly out of doors. A reader will like them best, I think, who reads them in similar circumstances—at least in a quiet room. They would be most favorably heard if read aloud into a kind of quietness that is not afforded by any public place. I hope that some readers will read them as they were written: slowly, and with more patience than effort.

I am an amateur poet, working for the love of the work and to my own satisfaction—which are two of the conditions of "self-employment," as I understand it. I belong to no school of poetry, but rather to my love for certain poems by other poets, some of whom, I am thankful to say, are my contemporaries.

I should say also that the poems printed here should be thought of as a series, not as a sequence. The poems are about moments when heart and mind are open and aware. Such moments, in my experience, are not sequent or consequent in the usual sense. Such a moment is not necessarily the cause or result of another such moment.

The dedication acknowledges two immeasurable debts: to Donald Hall, who has been a kind, exacting friend to these poems from the beginning; and to Kathleen Raine, whose work as poet, scholar, and editor has helped me probably more than I know.

This Day: An Introduction

The idea of the sabbath in these poems comes from Genesis 2:2: "And on the seventh day God ended his work which he had made; and he rested on the seventh day . . ." The sense of this day is transferred to humankind (by the fourth of the Ten Commandments) in Exodus 20:8-11: "Remember the sabbath day, to keep it holy. Six days shalt thou labour, and do all thy work: But the seventh day is the sabbath of the Lord thy God: in it thou shalt not do any work . . ."

On Sunday mornings I often attend a church in which I sometimes sat with my grandfather, in which I sometimes sit with my grandchildren, and in which my wife plays the piano. But I am a bad-weather churchgoer. When the weather is good, sometimes when it is only tolerable, I am drawn to the woods on the local hillsides or along the streams. The woodlands here are not "the forest primeval" or "wilderness areas." Nearly all are reforested old tobacco patches abandoned a lifetime or more ago, where you can still see the marks of cropland erosion now mostly healed or healing.

In such places, on the best of these sabbath days, I experience a lovely freedom from expectations—other people's and also my own. I go free from the tasks and intentions of my workdays, and so my mind becomes hospitable to unintended thoughts: to what I am very willing to call inspiration. The poems come incidentally or they do not come at all. If the Muse leaves me alone, I leave her alone. To be quiet, even wordless, in a good place is a better gift than poetry.

On those days and other days also, the idea of the sabbath has been on my mind. It is as rich and demanding an idea as any I know. The sabbath is the day, and the successive days honoring the day, when God rested after finishing the work of creation. This work was not finished, I think, in the sense of once and for all. It was finished by being given the power to exist and to continue, even to repair itself as it is now doing on the reforested hillsides of my home country.

We are to rest on the sabbath also, I have supposed, in order to understand that the providence or the productivity of the living world, the most essential work, continues while we rest. This work is entirely independent of our work, and is far more complex and wonderful than any work we have ever done or will ever do. It is more complex and wonderful than we will ever understand.

From the biblical point of view, the earth and our earthly livelihood are conditional gifts. We may possess the land given to us, that we are given to, only by remembering our intimate kinship with it. The condition of the people is indistinguishable ultimately from the condition of the land. Work that destroys the land, diminishing its ability to support life, is a great evil for which sooner or later the punishment is homelessness, hunger, and thirst. For some, the context of this thinking has shifted from religion to science, but the understanding of the land as a conditional gift has not changed.

The idea of the sabbath gains in meaning as it is brought out-of-doors and into a place where nature's principles of self-sustaining wholeness and health are still evident. In such a place – as never, for me, under a roof – the natural and the supernatural, the heavenly and the earthly, the soul and the body, the wondrous and the ordinary, all appear to occur together in the one fabric of creation. All stand both upon the earth and upon the fundamental miracle that where once was nothing now we have these creatures in this place on this day. In such a place one might expectably come to rest, with trust renewed in the creation's power to exist and to continue.

But how is a human being to come to rest in the presence of time, error, and mortality, in the midst of the demands of livelihood and civic responsibility, in knowing of all that human beings have done and are doing to damage the given world, and in knowing one's own complicity in that damage?

Nature of course includes damage as a part of her wholeness. Her creatures live only by the deaths of other creatures. Wind, flood, and fire are as much her means of world-making as birth, growth, maturity, death, and decay. She destroys and she heals. Her ways are cyclic, but she is absolutely original. She never exactly repeats herself, and this is the source equally of our grief and our delight. But Nature's damages are followed by her healings, though not necessarily on a human schedule or in human time. The "creative destruction" of industrialism, by contrast, implies no repayment of what we have taken, no healing, but is in effect a repudiation of our membership in the land-community.

The fundamental conflict of our time is that between the creaturely life of Nature's world and the increasingly mechanical life of modern humans. Among the poets of the twentieth century nobody was more aware of this contradiction than T. S. Eliot, who believed that "religion . . . implies a life in conformity to nature. It may be observed that the natural life and the supernatural life have a conformity to each other which neither has with the mechanistic life . . ." (*Christianity and Culture*, 48).

As for coming to rest, Eliot wrote:

> The endless cycle of idea and action,
> Endless invention, endless experiment,
> Brings knowledge of motion, but not of stillness . . .
>   (Choruses from "The Rock," lines 6-8.)

This quantitative endlessness, including also the idea of endless economic "growth," is clearly different from the inexhaustibility of Nature on her terms, and of goodness, beauty, and truth on ours. To rest, we must accept Nature's limits and our own. When we come to our limit, we must be still.

For anybody conscious of the history of the collision between the living world and the purposes of mechanistic humans, and of the marks and scars almost everywhere of that collision, heartbreak comes easy and rest comes hard. All rest partakes, consciously or not, of the sabbath. But the idea of sabbath rest, consciously understood and accepted, becomes an unexcusing standard by which to judge our history, our lives, and our work. And so the unintended thought on a Sunday walk, the thought invoked by the sabbath theme, does not dependably lead to rest. By disfigurements that our time imposes upon consciousness, by scars of bad history that mark the land, by sounds of machinery dominating the air, the mind may be returned to themes of loss, estrangement, and sorrow. That one is sometimes able, among the disturbances of the present world, to wander into some good and beautiful whereabouts of the woods, grow quiet, and come to rest is a gift, a wonder, and a kind of grace. Though associated with a particular day, this is a possibility that may present itself at any time.

The practical circumstance of these poems has been the mostly sloping farm in the Kentucky River valley where my wife and I have lived for nearly fifty years, where we brought up our children and helped to bring up our grandchildren, where for many years we raised most of our food and still are raising much of it, where we have gathered heating fuel from the woods and lately much of our electricity from solar collectors. My worrying about the ecological overdraft of the industrial economy has been repeatedly brought home by my efforts to care properly for pastures and woodlands on steep land that is quickly hurt and slow to heal.

My work as a writer is thus intimately related to my work as a marginal farmer. Because the two are connected and ongoing, this relationship has never been fixed. As these poems have accumulated over the years, their subjects have remained liable to disturbance and to change. As I have read through the pages of this new collection, I have been surprised by the sense they convey (at least to me) of my struggle to know what I have been doing in my work, my dwelling place, and this world.

For example, the project described in VI, 1982, was a somewhat experimental effort to establish, under the influence of J. Russell

Smith's *Tree Crops*, a sort of hillside savannah: trees above, pasture below. This effort was sound in principal and I learned a good deal from it, but after a few years I had to abandon it, mainly for want of time to keep it adequately fenced.

And when I quit mowing the pasture we call "the home hillside," I anticipated that it would soon be reclaimed by trees, as described in IV, 1990. My anticipation was wrong. I did not foresee that our ewe flock, continuing to graze that pasture in winter, would bite off the seedling trees, especially the hardwoods but also most of the cedars, and so preserve the grass.

I see also that my language has changed. In the earlier poems, I used the words "spirit" and "wild" conventionally and complacently. Later I became unhappy with both. I resolved, first, to avoid "spirit." This was not because I think the word itself is without meaning, but because I could no longer tolerate the dualism, often construed in sermons and such as a contest, of spirit and matter. I saw that once this division was made, spirit invariably triumphed to the detriment, to the actual and often irreparable damage, of matter and the material world. Dispensing with the word "spirit" clears the way to imagine a live continuity, in fact and value, between what we call "spiritual" and what we call "material."

As for "wild," I now think the word is misused. The longer I have lived and worked here among the noncommercial creatures of the woods and fields, the less I have been able to conceive of them as "wild." They plainly are going about their own domestic lives, finding or making shelter, gathering food, minding their health, raising their young, always well-adapted to their places. They are far better at domesticity than we industrial humans are. It became clear to me also that they think of us as wild, and that they are right. We are the ones who are undomesticated, barbarous, unrestrained, disorderly, extravagant, and out of control. They are our natural teachers, and we have learned too little from them. The woods itself, conventionally thought of as "wild," in fact is thought of and used as *home* by the creatures who are domesticated within it. In

II, 1995, I tried defining "wild," in a way that still seems fairly satisfactory. But when, in VIII, 2009, I was able finally to write of our habitat here as a "living place of many / lives, complexly domestic," I felt I had got past a major cultural obstruction.

In my efforts both to make these poems and to make some manner of peace between me and my dwelling place, I have constantly been instructed and encouraged by the work of agricultural and ecological scientists such as Liberty Hyde Bailey, F. H. King, J. Russell Smith, Albert Howard, Aldo Leopold, Stan Rowe, Wes Jackson, and John Todd, who have understood that, in any work of land use, the local ecosystem must be the model and measure. And my thoughts have returned again and again to the practical devotion to Nature in the poetry of Chaucer, Spenser, Shakespeare, Milton, and Pope.

. . . if he gather unto himself
his spirit and his breath;
All flesh shall perish together . . .

JOB 34: 14–15

The whole earth is at rest, and is
quiet: they break forth into singing.

ISAIAH 14:7

Imp ontar! do not charge most innocent Nature,
As if she would her children should be riotous
With her abundance. She, good cateress,
Means her provision only to the good,
That live according to her sober laws,
And holy dictate of spare Temperance.

JOHN MILTON, *Comus*

This Day

Sabbath Poems
Collected and New
1979–2013

Preface: From Sabbaths 2013

I

This is a poet of the river lands,
a lowdown man of the deepest
depth of the valley, where gravity gathers
the waters, the poisons, the trash,
where light comes late and leaves early.

From the window of his small room
the lowdown poet looks out. He watches
the river for ripples, flashes, signs
of beings rising in the undersurface dark,
or lightly swimming upon the flow,
or, for a minnow, descending the deeps
of the air to enter and shatter
forever their momentary reflections,
for the river is a place passing
through a passing place.

The poet, his window, and his poems
are creatures of the shore that the river
gnaws, dissolves, and carries away.
He is a tree of a sort, rooted
in the dark, aspiring to the light,
dependent on both. His poems
are leavings, sheddings, gathered
from the light, as it has come,
and offered to the dark, which he believes
must shine with sight,
with light, dark only to him.

II

Times will come as they must,
by necessity or his wish, when he leaves
his enclosure and his window,
his homescape of house and garden,
barn and pasture, the incarnate life
of his desire, thought, and daily work.
His grazing animals look up
to watch in silence as he departs.
He sets out at times without even
a path or any guidance other than knowledge
of the place and himself as they were
in time already past. He goes among trees,
climbing again the one hill of his life.
With his hand full of words he goes
into the wordless, wording it barely
in time as he passes. One by one he places
words, balancing on each
as on a small stone in the swift flow
in his anxious patience until
the next arrives, until he has come
at last again into presentiment
of the Real, the wholly real in its grand
composure, for which as before
he knows no word. And here again
he must stop. Here by luck or grace he may
find rest, which he has been seeking
all along. Sometimes by the time's flaws
and his own, he fails. And then
by luck or grace he will be given
another day to try again, to go maybe
yet farther before again he must stop.
He is a gatherer of fragments, a cobbler
of pieces. Piece by piece he tells
a story without end, for in the time

of this world no end can come.
It is the story of eternity's shining,
much shadowed, much put off,
in time. And time, however long, falls short.

I

I go among trees and sit still.
All my stirring becomes quiet
around me like circles on water.
My tasks lie in their places
where I left them, asleep like cattle.

Then what is afraid of me comes
and lives a while in my sight.
What it fears in me leaves me,
and the fear of me leaves it.
It sings, and I hear its song.

Then what I am afraid of comes.
I live for a while in its sight.
What I fear in it leaves it,
and the fear of it leaves me.
It sings, and I hear its song.

After days of labor,
mute in my consternations,
I hear my song at last,
and I sing it. As we sing,
the day turns, the trees move.

II

Another Sunday morning comes
And I resume the standing Sabbath
Of the woods, where the finest blooms
Of time return, and where no path

Is worn but wears its makers out
At last, and disappears in leaves
Of fallen seasons. The tracked rut
Fills and levels; here nothing grieves

In the risen season. Past life
Lives in the living. Resurrection
Is in the way each maple leaf
Commemorates its kind, by connection

Outreaching understanding. What rises
Rises into comprehension
And beyond. Even falling raises
In praise of light. What is begun

Is unfinished. And so the mind
That comes to rest among the bluebells
Comes to rest in motion, refined
By alteration. The bud swells,

Opens, makes seed, falls, is well,
Being becoming what it is:
Miracle and parable
Exceeding thought, because it is

Immeasurable; the understander
Encloses understanding, thus
Darkens the light. We can stand under
No ray that is not dimmed by us.

The mind that comes to rest is tended
In ways that it cannot intend:
Is borne, preserved, and comprehended
By what it cannot comprehend.

Your Sabbath, Lord, thus keeps us by
Your will, not ours. And it is fit
Our only choice should be to die
Into that rest, or out of it.

III

To sit and look at light-filled leaves
May let us see, or seem to see,
Far backward as through clearer eyes
To what unsighted hope believes:
The blessed conviviality
That sang Creation's seventh sunrise,

Time when the Maker's radiant sight
Made radiant every thing He saw,
And every thing He saw was filled
With perfect joy and life and light.
His perfect pleasure was sole law;
No pleasure had become self-willed.

For all His creatures were His pleasures
And their whole pleasure was to be
What He made them; they sought no gain
Or growth beyond their proper measures,
Nor longed for change or novelty.
The only new thing could be pain.

IV

The bell calls in the town
Where forebears cleared the shaded land
And brought high daylight down
To shine on field and trodden road.
I hear, but understand
Contrarily, and walk into the woods.
I leave labor and load,
Take up a different story.
I keep an inventory
Of wonders and of uncommercial goods.

I climb up through the field
That my long labor has kept clear.
Projects, plans unfulfilled
Waylay and snatch at me like briars,
For there is no rest here
Where ceaseless effort seems to be required,
Toil fails, and spirit tires
With flesh, because failure
And weariness are sure
In all that mortal wishing has inspired.

I go in pilgrimage
Across an old fenced boundary
To wildness without age
Where, in their long dominion,
The trees have been left free.
They call the soil here "Eden"—slants and steeps
Hard to stand straight up on
Even without a burden.
No more a perfect garden,
There's an immortal memory that it keeps.

I leave work's daily rule
And come here to this restful place
Where music stirs the pool
And from high stations of the air
Fall notes of wordless grace,
Strewn remnants of the primal Sabbath's hymn.
And I remember here
A tale of evil twined
With good, serpent and vine,
And innocence as evil's stratagem.

I let that go a while,
For it is hopeless to correct
By generations' toil,
And I let go my hopes and plans
That no toil can perfect.
There is no vision here but what is seen:
White bloom nothing explains
But a mute blessedness
Exceeding all distress,
The fresh light stained a hundred shades of green.

Uproar of wheel and fire
That has contained us like a cell
Opens and lets us hear
A stillness longer than all time
Where leaf and song fulfill
The passing light, pass with the light, return,
Renewed, as in a rhyme.
This is no human vision
Subject to our revision;
God's eye holds every leaf as light is worn.

Ruin is in place here:
The dead leaves rotting on the ground,
The live leaves in the air
Are gathered in a single dance
That turns them round and round.
The fox cub trots his almost pathless path
As silent as his absence.
These passings resurrect
A joy without defect,
The life that steps and sings in ways of death.

V

How many have relinquished
Breath, in grief or rage,
The victor and the vanquished
Named on the bitter page

Alike, or indifferently
Forgot—all that they did
Undone entirely.
The dust they stirred has hid

Their faces and their works,
Has settled, and lies still.
Nobody rests or shirks
Who must turn in time's mill.

They wind the turns of the mill
In house and field and town;
As grist is ground to meal
The grinders are ground down.

VI

What stood will stand, though all be fallen,
The good return that time has stolen.
Though creatures groan in misery,
Their flesh prefigures liberty
To end travail and bring to birth
Their new perfection in new earth.
At word of that enlivening
Let the trees of the woods all sing
And every field rejoice, let praise
Rise up out of the ground like grass.
What stood, whole in every piecemeal
Thing that stood, will stand though all
Fall—field and woods and all in them
Rejoin the primal Sabbath's hymn.

VII

What if, in the high, restful sanctuary
That keeps the memory of Paradise,
We're followed by the drone of history
And greed's poisonous fumes still burn our eyes?

Disharmony recalls us to our work.
From Heavenly work of light and wind and leaf
We must turn back into the peopled dark
Of our unraveling century, the grief

Of waste, the agony of haste and noise.
It is a hard return from Sabbath rest
To lifework of the fields, yet we rejoice,
Returning, less condemned in being blessed

By vision of what human work can make:
A harmony between forest and field,
The world as it was given for love's sake,
The world by love and loving work revealed

As given to our children and our Maker.
In that healed harmony the world is used
But not destroyed, the Giver and the taker
Joined, the taker blessed, in the unabused

Gift that nurtures and protects. Then workday
And Sabbath live together in one place.
Though mortal, incomplete, that harmony
Is our one possibility of peace.

When field and woods agree, they make a rhyme
That stirs in distant memory the whole
First Sabbath's song that no largess of time
Or hope or sorrow wholly can recall.

But harmony of earth is Heaven-made,
Heaven-making, is promise and is prayer,
A little song to keep us unafraid,
An earthly music magnified in air.

VIII

I go from the woods into the cleared field:
A place no human made, a place unmade
By human greed, and to be made again.
Where centuries of leaves once built by dying
A deathless potency of light and stone
And mold of all that grew and fell, the timeless
Fell into time. The earth fled with the rain,
The growth of fifty thousand years undone
In a few careless seasons, stripped to rock
And clay—a "new land," truly, that no race
Was ever native to, but hungry mice
And sparrows and the circling hawks, dry thorns
And thistles sent by generosity
Of new beginning. No Eden, this was
A garden once, a good and perfect gift;
Its possible abundance stood in it
As it then stood. But now what it might be
Must be foreseen, darkly, through many lives—
Thousands of years to make it what it was,
Beginning now, in our few troubled days.

IX

Enclosing the field within bounds
sets it apart from the boundless
of which it was, and is, a part,
and places it within care.
The bounds of the field bind
the mind to it. A bride
adorned, the field now wears
the green veil of a season's
abounding. Open the gate!
Open it wide, that time
and hunger may come in.

X

Whatever is foreseen in joy
Must be lived out from day to day,
Vision held open in the dark
By our ten thousand days of work.
Harvest will fill the barn; for that
The hand must ache, the face must sweat.

And yet no leaf or grain is filled
By work of ours; the field is tilled
And left to grace. That we may reap,
Great work is done while we're asleep.

When we work well, a Sabbath mood
Rests on our day, and finds it good.

XI

To long for what can be fulfilled in time
Foredooms the body to the use of light,
Light into light returning, as the stream

Of days flows downward through us into night,
And into light and life and time to come.
This is the way of death: loss of what might

Have been in what must come to be, light's sum
Lost in the having, having to forego.
The year drives on toward what it will become.

In answer to their names called long ago
The creatures all have risen and replied
Year after year, each toward the distant glow

Of its perfection in all, glorified;
I have failed, That after year they all disperse
As the leaves fall, and not to be denied

The frost falls on the grass as by a curse.
The leaves flame, fall, and carry down their light
By a hard justice in the universe

Against all fragmentary things. Their flight
Sends them downward into the dark, unseen
Empowerment of a universal right

That brings them back to air and light again,
One grand motion, implacable, sublime.
The calling of all creatures is design.

We long for what can be fulfilled in time,
Though death is in the cost. There is a craving
As in delayed completion of a rhyme

To know what may be had by loss of having,
To see what loss of time will make of seed
In earth or womb, dark come to light, the saving

Of what was lost in what will come—repaid
In the invisible pattern that will mark
Whatever of the passing light is made.

Choosing the light in which the sun is dark,
The stars dark, and all mortal vision blind—
That puts us out of thought and out of work,

And dark by day, in heart dark, dark in mind,
Mistaking for a song our lonely cry,
We turn in wrongs of love against our kind;

The fall returns. Our deeds and days gone by
Take root, bear fruit, are carried on, in faith
Or fault, through deaths all mortal things must die,

The deaths of time and pain, and death's own death
In full-filled light and song, final Sabbath.

XII

To long for what eternity fulfills
Is to forsake the light one has, or wills
To have, and go into the dark, to wait
What light may come — no light perhaps, the dark
Insinuates. And yet the dark conceals
All possibilities: thought, word, and light,
Air, water, earth, motion, and song, the arc
Of lives through light, eyesight, hope, rest, and work —

And death, the narrow gate each one must pass
Alone, as some have gone past every guess
Into the woods by a path lost to all
Who look back, gone past light and sound of day
Into grief's wordless catalogue of loss.
As the known life is given up, birdcall
Become the only language of the way,
The leaves all shine with sudden light, and stay

1980

I

What hard travail God does in death!
He strives in sleep, in our despair,
And all flesh shudders underneath
The nightmare of His sepulcher.

The earth shakes, grinding its deep stone;
All night the cold wind heaves and prics;
Creation strains sinew and bone
Against the dark door where He lies.

The stem bent, pent in seed, grows straight
And stands. Pain breaks in song. Surprising
The merely dead, graves fill with light
Like opened eyes. He rests in rising.

II

The eager dog lies strange and still
Who roamed the woods with me;
Then while I stood or climbed the hill
Or sat under a tree,

Awaiting what more time might say,
He thrashed in undergrowth,
Pursuing what he scared away,
Made ruckus for us both.

He's dead; I go more quiet now,
Stillness added to me
By time and sorrow, mortal law,
By loss of company

That his new absence has made new.
Though it must come by doom,
This quiet comes by kindness too,
And brings me nearer home,

For as I walk the wooded land
The morning of God's mercy,
Beyond the work of mortal hand,
Seen by more than I see,

The quiet deer look up and wait,
Held still in quick of grace.
And I wait, stop footstep and thought.
We stand here face to face.

III

Great deathly powers have passed:
The black and bitter cold, the wind
That broke and felled strong trees, the rind
Of ice that held at last

Even the fleshly heart
In cold that made it seem a stone.
And now there comes again the one
First Sabbath light, the Art

That unruled, uninvoked,
Unknown, makes new again and heals,
Restores heart's flesh so that it feels
Anew the old deadlocked

Goodness of its true home
That it will lose again and mourn
Remembering the year reborn
In almost perfect bloom

In almost shadeless wood,
Sweet air that neither burned nor chilled
In which the tenderest flowers prevailed,
The light made flesh and blood.

IV

The frog with lichened back and golden thigh
Sits still, almost invisible
On leafed and lichened stem,
Invisibility
Its sign of being at home
There in its given place, and well.

The warbler with its quivering striped throat
Would live almost beyond my sight,
Almost beyond belief,
But for its double note –
Among high leaves a leaf,
At ease, at home in air and light.

And I, through woods and fields, through fallen days,
Am passing to where I belong:
At home, at ease, and well,
In Sabbaths of this place
Almost invisible,
Toward which I go from song to song.

V

Six days of work are spent
To make a Sunday quiet
That Sabbath may return.
It comes in unconcern;
We cannot earn or buy it.
Suppose rest is not sent
Or comes and goes unknown,
The light, unseen, unshown.
Suppose the day begins
In wrath at circumstance,
Or anger at one's friends
In vain self-innocence
False to the very light,
Breaking the sun in half,
Or anger at oneself
Whose controverting will
Would have the sun stand still.
The world is lost in loss
Of patience; the old curse
Returns, and is made worse
As newly justified.
In hopeless fret and fuss,
In rage at worldly plight
Creation is defied,
All order is unpropped,
All light and singing stopped.

VI

The intellect so ravenous to know
And in its knowing hold the very light,
Disclosing what is so and what not so,

Must finally know the dark, which is its right
And liberty; it's blind in what it sees.
Bend down, go in by this low door, despite

The thorn and briar that bar the way. The trees
Are young here in the heavy undergrowth
Upon an old field worn out by disease

Of human understanding; greed and sloth
Did bad work that this thicket now conceals,
Work lost to rain or ignorance or both.

The young trees make a darkness here that heals,
And here the forms of human thought dissolve
Into the living shadow that reveals

All orders made by mortal hand or love
Or thought come to a margin of their kind,
Are lost in order we are ignorant of,

Which stirs great fear and sorrow in the mind.
The field, if it will thrive, must do so by
Exactitude of thought, by skill of hand,

And by the clouded mercy of the sky;
It is a mortal clarity between
Two darks, of Heaven and of earth. The why

Of it is *our* measure. Seen and unseen,
Its causes shape it as it is, a while.
O bent by fear and sorrow, now bend down,

Leave word and argument, be dark and still,
And come into the joy of healing shade.
Rest from your work. Be still and dark until

You grow as unopposing, unafraid
As the young trees, without thought or belief;
Until the shadow Sabbath light has made

Shudders, breaks open, shines in every leaf.

I

Here where the world is being made,
No human hand required,
A man may come, somewhat afraid
Always, and somewhat tired,

For he comes ignorant and alone
From work and worry of
A human place, in soul and bone
The ache of human love.

He may come and be still, not go
Toward any chosen aim
Or stay for what he thinks is so,
Setting aside his claim

On all things fallen in his plight,
His mind may move with leaves,
Wind-shaken, in and out of light,
And live as the light lives,

And live as the Creation sings
In covert, two clear notes,
And waits; then two clear answerings
Come from more distant throats —

May live a while with light, shaking
In high leaves, or delayed
In halts of song, submit to making,
The shape of what is made.

I

Dream ended, I went out, awake
To new snow fallen in the dark,
Stainless on road and field, no track
Yet printed on my day of work.

I heard the wild ones muttering,
Assent their dark arrival made
At dawn, gray dawn on dawn-gray wing
Outstretched, shadowless in that shade,

Down from high distances arrived
Within the shelter of the hill;
The river shuddered as they cleaved
Its surface, floated, and were still.

II

Here where the dark-sourced stream brims up,
Reflecting daylight, making sound
In its stepped fall from cup to cup
Of tumbled rocks, singing its round

From cloud to sea to cloud, I climb
The deer road through the leafless trees
Under a wind that batters limb
On limb, still roaring as it has

Two nights and days, cold in slow spring.
But ancient song in a wild throat
Recalls itself and starts to sing
In storm-cleared light; and the bloodroot,

Twinleaf, and rue anemone
Among bare shadows rise, keep faith
With what they have been and will be
Again: frail stem and leaf, mere breath

Of white and starry bloom, each form
Recalling itself to its place
And time. Give thanks, for no windstorm
Or human wrong has altered this,

The forfeit Garden that recalls
Itself here, where both we and it
Belong; no act or thought rebels
In this brief Sabbath now, time fit

To be eternal. Such a bliss
Of bloom's no ornament, but root
And light, a saving loveliness,
Starred firmament here underfoot.

III

The pasture, bleached and cold two weeks ago,
Begins to grow in the spring light and rain;
The new grass trembles under the wind's flow.
The flock, barn-weary, comes to it again,
New to the lambs, a place their mothers know,
Welcoming, bright, and savory in its green,
So fully does the time recover it.
Nibbles of pleasure go all over it.

IV

Thrush song, stream song, holy love
That flows through earthly forms and folds,
The song of Heaven's Sabbath fleshed
In throat and ear, in stream and stone,
A grace living here as we live,
Move my mind now to that which holds
Things as they change.
                              The warmth has come.
The doors have opened. Flower and song
Embroider ground and air, lead me
Beside the healing field that waits;
Growth, death, and a restoring form
Of human use will make it well.
But I go on, beyond, higher
In the hill's fold, forget the time
I come from and go to, recall
This grove left out of all account,
A place enclosed in song.
                              Design
Now falls from thought. I go amazed
Into the maze of a design
That mind can follow but not know,
Apparent, plain, and yet unknown,
The outline lost in earth and sky.
What form wakens and rumples this?
Be still. A man who seems to be
A gardener rises out of the ground,
Stands like a tree, shakes off the dark,
The bluebells opening at his feet,
The light a figured cloth of song.

V

To Mary

A child unborn, the coming year
Grows big within us, dangerous,
And yet we hunger as we fear
For its increase: the blunted bud

To free the leaf to have its day,
The unborn to be born. The ones
Who are to come are on their way,
And though we stand in mortal good

Among our dead, we turn in doom
In joy to welcome them, stirred by
That Ghost who stirs in seed and tomb,
Who brings the stones to parenthood.

VI

To Den

We have walked so many times, my boy,
over these old fields given up
to thicket, have thought
and spoken of their possibilities,
theirs and ours, ours and theirs the same,
so many times, that now when I walk here
alone, the thought of you goes with me;
my mind reaches toward yours
across the distance and through time.

No mortal mind's complete within itself,
but minds must speak and answer,
as ours must, on the subject of this place,
our history here, summoned
as we are to the correction
of old wrong in this soil, thinned
and broken, and in our minds.

You have seen on these gullied slopes
the piles of stones mossy with age,
dragged out of furrows long ago
by men now names on stones,
who cleared and broke these fields,
saw them go to ruin, learned nothing
from the trees they saw return
to hold the ground again.

But here is a clearing we have made
at no cost to the world
and to our gain—a *re*-clearing
after forty years: the thicket
cut level with the ground,

grasses and clovers sown
into the last year's fallen leaves,
new pasture coming to the sun
as the woods plants, lovers of shade,
give way: change made
without violence to the ground.

At evening birdcall
flares at the woods' edge;
flight arcs into the opening
before nightfall.

Out of disordered history
a little coherence, a pattern
comes, like the steadying
of a rhythm on a drum, melody
coming to it from time
to time, waking over it,
as from a bird at dawn
or nightfall, the long outline
emerging through the momentary,
as the hill's hard shoulder
shows through trees
when the leaves fall.

The field finds its source
in the old forest, in the thicket
that returned to cover it,
in the dark wilderness of its soil,
in the dispensations of the sky,
in our time, in our minds—
the righting of what was done wrong.

Wrong was easy; gravity helped it.
Right is difficult and long.
In choosing what is difficult

we are free, the mind too
making its little flight
out from the shadow into the clear
in time between work and sleep.

There are two healings: nature's,
and ours and nature's. Nature's
will come in spite of us, after us,
over the graves of its wasters, as it comes
to the forsaken fields. The healing
that is ours and nature's will come
if we are willing, if we are patient,
if we know the way, if we will do the work.
My father's father, whose namesake
you are, told my father this, he told me,
and I am telling you: we make
this healing, the land's and ours:
it is our possibility. We may keep
this place, and be kept by it.
There is a mind of such an artistry
that grass will follow it,
and heal and hold, feed beasts
who will feed us and feed the soil.

Though we invite, this healing comes
in answer to another voice than ours;
a strength not ours returns
out of death beginning in our work.

Though the spring is late and cold,
though uproar of greed
and malice shudders in the sky,
pond, stream, and treetop raise
their ancient songs;
the robin molds her mud nest

with her breast; the air
is bright with breath
of bloom, wise loveliness that asks
nothing of the season but to be.

VII

The clearing rests in song and shade.
It is a creature made
By old light held in soil and leaf,
By human joy and grief,
By human work,
Fidelity of sight and stroke,
By rain, by water on
The parent stone.

We join our work to Heaven's gift,
Our hope to what is left,
That field and woods at last agree
In an economy
Of widest worth.
High Heaven's Kingdom come on earth.
Imagine Paradise.
O dust, arise!

VIII

Our household for the time made right,
All right around us on the hill
For time and for this time, tonight,
Two kernels folded in one shell,

We're joined in sleep beyond desire
To one another and to time,
Whatever time will take or spare,
Forest, field, house, and hollow room

All joined to us, to darkness joined,
All barriers down, and we are borne
Darkly, by thoroughfares unsigned
Toward light we come in time to learn,

In faith no better sighted yet
Than when we plighted first by hope,
By vows more solemn than we thought,
Ourselves to this combining sleep

A quarter century ago,
Lives given to each other and
To time, to lives we did not know
Already given, heart and hand.

Would I come to this time this way
Again, now that I know, confess
So much, knowing I cannot say
More now than then what will be? Yes.

May 29, 1957   May 29, 1982

IX

(Sunday, July 4)

Hail to the forest born again,
that by neglect, the American benevolence,
has returned to semi-virginity, graceful
in the putrid air, the corrosive rain,
the ash-fall of Heaven-invading fire —
our time's genius to mine the light
of the world's ancient buried days
to make it poisonous in the air.
Light and greed together make a smudge
that stifles and blinds. But here
the light of Heaven's sun descends,
stained and mingled with its forms,
heavy trunk and limb, light leaf and wing,
that we must pray for clarity to see,
not raw sources, symbols, worded powers,
but fellow presences, independent, called
out of nothing by no word of ours,
blessèd, here with us.

X

The dark around us, come,
Let us meet here together,
Members one of another,
Here in our holy room,

Here on our little floor,
Here in the daylit sky,
Rejoicing mind and eye,
Rejoining known and knower,

Light, leaf, foot, hand, and wing,
Such order as we know,
One household, high and low,
And all the earth shall sing.

I

In a crease of the hill
under the light,
out of the wind,
as warmth, bloom, and song
return, lady, I think of you,
and of myself with you.
What are we but forms
of the self-acknowledging
light that brings us
warmth and song from time
to time? Lip and flower,
hand and leaf, tongue
and song, what are we but welcomers
of that ancient joy, always
coming, always passing?
Mayapples rising
out of old time, leaves
folded down around
the stems, as if for flight,
flower bud folded in
unfolding leaves, what
are we but hosts
of times, of all
the Sabbath morning shows,
the light that finds it good.

II

The year relents, and free
Of work, I climb again
To where the old trees wait,
Time out of mind. I hear
Traffic down on the road,
Engines high overhead.
And then a quiet comes,
A cleft in time, silence
Of metal moved by fire;
The air holds little voices,
Titmice and chickadees,
Feeding through the treetops
Among the new small leaves,
Calling again to mind
The grace of circumstance,
Sabbath economy
In which all thought is song,
All labor is a dance.
The world is made at rest,
In ease of gravity.
I hear the ancient theme
In low world-shaping song
Sung by the falling stream.
Here where a rotting log
Has slowed the flow: a shelf
Of dark soil, level laid
Above the tumbled stone.
Roots fasten it in place.
It will be here a while;
What holds it here decays.
A richness from above,
Brought down, is held, and holds

A little while in flow.
Stem and leaf grow from it.
At cost of death, it has
A life. Thus falling founds,
Unmaking makes the world.

III

Now though the season warms
The woods inherits harms
Of human enterprise.
Our making shakes the skies
And taints the atmosphere.
We have ourselves to fear.
We burn the world to live;
Our living blights the leaf.

A clamor high above
Entered the shadowed grove,
Withdrew, was still, and then
The water thrush began
The song that is a prayer,
A form made in the air,
That all who live here pray,
The Sabbath of our day.

May our kind live to breathe
Air worthy of the breath
Of all singers that sing
In joy of their making,
Light of the risen year,
Songs worthy of the ear
Of breathers worth their air,
Of workers worth their hire.

IV

Who makes a clearing makes a work of art,
The true world's Sabbath trees in festival
Around it. And the stepping stream, a part
Of Sabbath also, flows past, by its fall
Made musical, making the hillslope by
Its fall, and still at rest in falling, song
Rising. The field is made by hand and eye,
By daily work, by hope outreaching wrong,
And yet the Sabbath, parted, still must stay
In the dark mazings of the soil no hand
May light, the great Life, broken, make its way
Along the stemmy footholds of the ant.
    Bewildered in our timely dwelling place,
    Where we arrive by work, we stay by grace.

I

Over the river in loud flood,
in the wind deep and broad
under the unending sky, pair
by pair, the swallows again,
with tender exactitude,
play out their line
in arcs laid on the air,
as soon as made, not there.

II

A tired man leaves his labor, felt
In every ligament, to walk
Alone across the new-mowed field,
And at its bound, the last cut stalk,

He takes a road much overgone
In time by bearers of his name,
Though now where foot and hoof beat stone
And passed to what their toil became,

Trees stand that in their long leaf-fall,
Untroubled on forgiving ground,
Have buried the sledged stone with soil
So that his passing makes no sound.

He turns aside, and joins his quiet
Forebears in absence from that way.
He passes through the dappled light
And shadow that the breeze makes sway

Upon him and around him as
He goes. Within the day's design
The leaves sway, darkly, or ablaze
Around their edges with a line

Of fire caught from the sun. He steps
Amid a foliage of song
No tone of which has passed his lips.
Watching, silent, he shifts among

The shiftings of the day, himself
A shifting of the day's design
Whose outline is in doubt, unsafe,
And dark. One time, less learned in pain,

He thought the earth was firm, his own,
But now he knows that all not raised
By fire, by water is brought down.
The slope his fields lie on is poised

Above the river in mere air,
The breaking forewall of a wave,
And everything he has made there
Floats lightly on that fall. To save

What passes is a passing hope
Within the day's design outlawed.
His passing now has brought him up
Into a place not reached by road,

Beyond all history that he knows,
Where trees like great saints stand in time,
Eternal in their patience. Loss
Has rectified the songs that come

Into this columned room, and he
Only in silence, nothing in hand,
Comes here. A generosity
Is here by which the fallen stand.

In history many-named, in time
Nameless, this amplitude conveys
The answering to the asking rhyme
Among confusions that dispraise

The membering name that Adam spoke
By gift, and then heard parceled out
Among all fallen things that croak
And cry and sing and curse and shout.

The foliage opens like a cloud.
At rest high on the valley side,
Silent, the man looks at the loud
World: road and farm, his daily bread,

His beasts, his garden, and his barns,
His trees, the white walls of his house,
Whose lives and hopes he knows. He yearns
Toward all his work has joined. What has

He by his making made but home,
A present help by passing grace
Allowed to creatures of his name
Here in this passing time and place?

III

The crop must drink; we move the pipe
To draw the water back in time
To fall again upon the field,
So that the harvest may grow ripe,
The year complete its ancient rhyme
With other years, and a good yield
Complete our human hope. And this
Is Sunday work, necessity
Depriving us of needed rest.
Yet this necessity is less,
Being met, not by one, but three.
Neighbors, we make this need our feast.

IV

The summer ends, and it is time
To face another way. Our theme
Reversed, we harvest the last row
To store against the cold, undo
The garden that will be undone.
We grieve under the weakened sun
To see all earth's green fountains dried,
And fallen all the works of light.
You do not speak, and I regret
This downfall of the good we sought
As though the fault were mine. I bring
The plow to turn the shattering
Leaves and bent stems into the dark,
From which they may return. At work,
I see you leaving our bright land,
The last cut flowers in your hand.

V

Estranged by distance, he relearns
The way to quiet not his own,
The light at rest on tree and stone,
The high leaves falling in their turns,

Spiraling through the air made gold
By their slow fall. Bright on the ground,
They wait their darkening, commend
To coming light the light they hold.

His own long comedown from the air
Complete, safe home again, absence
Withdrawing from him tense by tense
In presence of the resting year,

Blessing and blessed in this result
Of times not blessed, now he has risen
He walks in quiet beyond division
In surcease of his own tumult.

I

Not again in this flesh will I see
the old trees stand here as they did,
weighty creatures made of light, delight
of their making straight in them and well,
whatever blight our blindness was or made,
however thought or act might fail.

The burden of absence grows, and I pay
daily the grief I owe to love
for women and men, days and trees
I will not know again. Pray
for the world's light thus borne away.
Pray for the little songs that wake and move,

For comfort as these lights depart,
recall again the angels of the thicket,
columbine aerial in the whelming tangle,
song drifting down, light rain, day
returning in song, the lordly Art
piecing out its humble way.

Though blindness may yet detonate in light,
ruining all, after all the years, great right
subsumed at last in paltry wrong,
what do we know? Still
the Presence that we come into with song
is here, shaping the seasons of His wild will.

II

A gracious Sabbath stood here while they stood
Who gave our rest a haven.
Now fallen, they are given
To labor and distress.
These times we know much evil, little good
To steady us in faith
And comfort when our losses press
Hard on us, and we choose,
In panic or despair or both,
To keep what we will lose.

For we are fallen like the trees, our peace
Broken, and so we must
Love where we cannot trust,
Trust where we cannot know,
And must await the wayward-coming grace
That joins living and dead,
Taking us where we would not go —
Into the boundless dark.
When what was made has been unmade
The Maker comes to His work.

III

Awaked from the persistent dream
Of human chaos come again,
I walk in the lamed woods, the light
Brought down by felling of great trees,
And in the rising thicket where
The shadow of old grace returns.
Leaf shadows tremble on light leaves,
A lighter foliage of song
Among them, the wind's thousand tongues,
And songs of birds. Beams reaching down
Into the shadow swirl and swarm
With gleaming traffic of the air,
Bright grains of generative dust
And winged intelligences. Among
High maple leaves a spider's wheel
Shines, work of finest making made
Touchingly in the dark.
                          The dark
Again has prayed the light to come
Down into it, to animate
And move it in its heaviness.

So what was still and dark wakes up,
Becomes intelligent, moves, names
Itself by hunger and by kind,
Walks, swims, flies, cries, calls, speaks, or sings.
We all are praising, praying to
The light we are, but cannot know.

IV

The fume and shock and uproar
of the internal combustion of America
recede, the last vacationers gone
back to the life that drives away from home.

Bottles and wrappers of expensive
cheap feasts ride the quieted current
toward the Gulf of Mexico.

And now the breeze comes down
from the hill, the kingfisher returns
to the dead limb of the sycamore,
the swallows feed in the air
over the water.

        A muskrat draws his V
under the lowhanging willows.
In clear shallows near the rocks
tiny fish flicker and soar. A dove
sweetens the distance with his call.

Out of the frenzy of an August Sunday
the Sabbath comes. The valley glows.
A raincrow flies across the river
into the shadowy leaves. The dark falls.

V

How long does it take to make the woods?
As long as it takes to make the world.
The woods is present as the world is, the presence
of all its past, and of all its time to come.
It is always finished, it is always being made, the act
of its making forever greater than the act of its destruction.
It is a part of eternity, for its end and beginning
belong to the end and beginning of all things,
the beginning lost in the end, the end in the beginning.

What is the way to the woods, how do you go there?
By climbing up through the six days' field,
kept in all the body's years, the body's
sorrow, weariness, and joy. By passing through
the narrow gate on the far side of that field
where the pasture grass of the body's life gives way
to the high, original standing of the trees
By coming into the shadow, the shadow
of the grace of the strait way's ending,
the shadow of the mercy of light.

Why must the gate be narrow?
Because you cannot pass beyond it burdened.
To come in among these trees you must leave behind
the six days' world, all of it, all of its plans and hopes.
You must come without weapon or tool, alone,
expecting nothing, remembering nothing,
into the ease of sight, the brotherhood of eye and leaf.

VI

Life forgives its depredations;
new-shaped by loss, goes on.
Luther Penn, our neighbor
still in our minds, will not
come down to the creek mouth to fish
in April anymore. The year
ripens. Leaves fall. In openings
where old trees were cut down,
showing the ground to the sky,
snakeroot blooms white,
giving shine unto the world.
Ant and beetle scuttle through
heroic passages, go to dust;
their armor tumbles in the mold.
Broad wings enter the grove, fold
and are still, open and go.

VII

The winter wren is back, quick
Among the treeroots by the stream,
Feeding from stem to stone to stick,
And in his late return the rhyme

Of years again completes itself.
He makes his work a kind of play.
He pauses on a little shelf
Of rock, says "Tick!" and flirts away,

Too busy in that other world
His hungry vision brings to sight
To be afraid. He makes a gnarled
Root graceful with his airy weight,

Breathes in the great informing Breath,
Made little in his wing and eye,
And breathes it out again in deft
Bright links of song, his clarity.

I

Slowly, slowly, they return
To the small woodland let alone:
Great trees, outspreading and upright,
Apostles of the living light.

Patient as stars, they build in air
Tier after tier a timbered choir,
Stout beams upholding weightless grace
Of song, a blessing on this place.

They stand in waiting all around,
Uprisings of their native ground,
Downcomings of the distant light;
They are the advent they await.

Receiving sun and giving shade,
Their life's a benefaction made,
And is a benediction said
Over the living and the dead.

In fall their brightened leaves, released,
Fly down the wind, and we are pleased
To walk on radiance, amazed.
O light come down to earth, be praised!

I

Coming to the woods' edge
on my Sunday morning walk,
I stand resting a moment beside
a ragged half-dead wild plum
in bloom, its perfume
a moment enclosing me,
and standing side by side
with the old broken blooming tree,
I almost understand,
I almost recognize as a friend
the great impertinence of beauty
that comes even to the dying,
even to the fallen, without reason
sweetening the air.

              I walk on,
distracted by a letter accusing me
of distraction, which distracts me
only from the hundred things
that would otherwise distract me
from this whiteness, lightness,
sweetness in the air. The mind
is broken by the thousand
calling voices it is always too late
to answer, and that is why it yearns
for some hard task, lifelong, longer
than life, to concentrate it
and to make it whole.

But where is the all-welcoming,
all-consecrating Sabbath
that would do the same? Where
the quietness of the heart
and the eye's clarity
that would be a friend's reply
to the white-blossoming plum tree?

II

I climb up through the thicket,
a bird's song somewhere within it,
the singer unfound within the song
resounding within itself and around
itself; it might come from anywhere,
from everywhere, the whole air
vibrant with it, every leaf a tongue.

❦

I reach the last stand in my going
of woodland never felled, a little patch
of trees on ground too poor to plow, spared
the belittlement of human intention
from time before human thought. They bring
that time to mind: their long standing, and
our longing to understand. But a man
Is small before those who have stood so long.
He stands under them, looks up, sees, knows,
and knows that he does not know.

❦

Explanations topple into their events,
merely other events, smaller and less
significant. They disappear, or die away
like little cries at sundown, and the old trees
receive the night again in dignity
and patience, present beyond the complex
lineages of cause and effect, each one
lost to us in what it is. For us, the privilege
is only to see, within the long shade,
the present standing of what has come and is

to come: the straight trunks aspiring
between earth and sky, bearing upon all years
the year's new leaves.

✦

                    Or we may see
this valley as from above and outside,
as from a distance off in time, as Cézanne
might have seen it: the light
stopped, at rest in its scintillation
on the bright strokes of the leaves
also at rest, sight and light entering
from the same direction, so that we see it
shadowless, for all time, forever.

✦

I come to a little bench, a mere shelf
of the slope, where four deer slept the night,
and I lie down in the deer's bed
and, warm in my old jacket in the cold
morning of late April, sleep a sleep as dark
and vast as the deer slept, or as the dead sleep,
simple and dreamless in their graves,
awaiting the dawn that will stand them
timeless as they stood in time, and at last
open my eyes to the bright sky, the luminous
small new leaves unfolding.

III

And now the lowland grove is down, the trees
Fallen that had unearthly power to please
The earthly eye, and gave unearthly solace
To minds grown quiet in that quiet place.
To see them standing was to know a prayer
Prayed to the Holy Spirit in the air
By that same Spirit dwelling in the ground.
The wind in their high branches gave the sound
Of air replying to that prayer. The rayed
Imperial light sang in the leaves it made.

To live as mourner of a human friend
Is but to understand the common end
Told by the steady counting in the wrist.
For though the absent friend is mourned and missed
At every pulse, it is a human loss
In human time made well; our grief will bless
At last the dear lost flesh and breath; it will
Grow quiet as the body in the hill.

To live to mourn an ancient woodland, known
Always, loved with an old love handed down,
That is a grief that will outlast the griever,
Grief as landmark, grief as a wearing river
That in its passing stays, biding in rhyme
Of year with year, time with returning time,
As though beyond the grave the soul will wait
In long unrest the shaping of the light
In branch and bole through centuries that prepare
This ground to pray again its finest prayer.

IV

May what I've written here
In sleepless grief and dread
Live in my children's ears
To warn them of their need
And ask them to forbear
In time when I am dead

So they may look and see
For past and future's sake
The terms of victory
They cannot win or take
Except by charity
Toward what they cannot make.

V

And now the remnant groves grow bright with praise.
They light around me like an old man's days.

VI

Remembering that it happened once,
We cannot turn away the thought,
As we go out, cold, to our barns
Toward the long night's end, that we
Ourselves are living in the world
It happened in when it first happened,
That we ourselves, opening a stall
(A latch thrown open countless times
Before), might find them breathing there,
Foreknown: the Child bedded in straw,
The mother kneeling over Him,
The husband standing in belief
He scarcely can believe, in light
That lights them from no source we see,
An April morning's light, the air
Around them joyful as a choir.
We stand with one hand on the door,
Looking into another world
That is this world, the pale daylight
Coming just as before, our chores
To do, the cattle all awake,
Our own white frozen breath hanging
In front of us; and we are here
As we have never been before,
Sighted as not before, our place
Holy, although we knew it not.

I

Now I have reached the age
of judgment giving sorrow
that many men have come to,
the verdict of regret,
remembering the world
once better than it is,
my old walkways beneath
the vanished trees, and friends
lost now in loss of trust.

And I recall myself
more innocent than I am,
gone past coming back
in the history of Haw,
except Christ dead and risen
in my own flesh shall judge,
condemn, and then forgive.

II

It is the destruction of the world
in our own lives that drives us
half insane, and more than half.
To destroy that which we were given
in trust: how will we bear it?
It is our own bodies that we give
to be broken, our bodies
existing before and after us
in clod and cloud, worm and tree,
that we, driving or driven, despise
in our greed to live, our haste
to die. To have lost, wantonly,
the ancient forests, the vast grasslands
is our madness, the presence
in our very bodies of our grief.

III

Another year has returned us
to the day of our marriage
thirty-one years ago. Many times
we have known, and again forgot
in our cruel separateness,
that making touch that feelingly
persuades us what we are:
one another's and many others',
brought together as by a music
of singing birds hidden among
the leaves, or the memory of
small flowers in the dark grass.
How strange to think of children
yet to come, into whose making we
will be made, who will not know us
even so little as we know
ourselves, who have already gone
so far beyond our own recall.

IV

·The world of machines is running
Beyond the world of trees
Where only a leaf is turning
In a small high breeze.

V

Always in the distance
the sound of cars is passing
on the road, that simplest form
going only two ways,
both ways away. And I
have been there in that going.

But now I rest and am
apart, a part of the form
of the woods always arriving
from all directions home,
this cell of wild sound,
the hush of the trees, singers
hidden among the leaves—

a form whose history is old,
needful, unknown, and bright
as the history of the stars
that tremble in the sky at night
like leaves of a great tree.

I

In early morning we awaken from
The sound of engines running in the night,
And then we start the engines of the day.
We speed away into the fading light.

Nowhere is any sound but of our going
On roads strung everywhere with humming wire.
Nowhere is there an end except in smoke.
This is the world that we have set on fire.

This is the promised burning, darkening
Our light of hope and putting out the sun,
Blighting the leaf, the stream—and blesséd are
The dead who died before this time began.

Blesséd the dead who have escaped in time
The twisted metal and the fractured stone,
The technobodies of the hopeless cure.
Now, to the living, only grief has shown

The little yellow of the violet
Risen again out of the dead year's leaves,
And grief alone is measure of the love
That only lives by rising out of graves.

II

The old oak wears new leaves.
It stands for many lives.
Within its veil of green
A singer sings unseen.
Again the living come
To light, and are at home.
And Edward Abbey's gone.
I pass a cairn of stone
Two arm-lengths long and wide
Piled on the steep hillside
By plowmen years ago.
Now oaks and hickories grow
Where the steel coulter passed.
Where human striving ceased
The Sabbath of the trees
Returns and stands and is.
The leaves shake in the wind.
I think of that dead friend
Here where he never came
Except by thought and name;
I praise the joyous rage
That justified his page.
He would have liked this place
Where spring returns with solace
Of bloom in a dark time,
Larkspur and columbine.
The flute song of the thrush
Sounds in the underbrush.

III   SANTA CLARA VALLEY

For Jim Powell

I walked the deserted prospect of the modern mind
where nothing lived or happened that had not been foreseen.
What had been foreseen was the coming of the Stranger with
    Money.
What had been before had been destroyed: the salt marsh
of unremembered time, the remembered homestead, orchard,
    and pasture.
A new earth had appeared in place of the old, made entirely
according to plan. New palm trees stood all in a row, new pines
all in a row, confined in cement to keep them from straying.

New buildings, built to seal and preserve the inside
against the outside, stood in the blatant outline of their purpose
in the ungraced air and light. Inside them
were sealed cool people, the foreseen ones, who did not look
or go in any way that they did not intend,
waited upon by lesser people, trained in servility, who begged
of the ones who had been foreseen: "Is everything
all right, sir? Have you enjoyed your dinner, sir?"

The highest good of that place was the control of temperature
and light, the next was to touch or know or say
or see no thing that had not been foreseen.
A small human understanding had arrayed itself
there without limit, had cast its grid upon the sky,
the stars, the rising and the setting sun.
I could not see past it but to its ruin.

I walked that desert of unremitting purpose, remembering
another valley where bodies and events took place and form
not always foreseen by humans, where all the land had not yet
been consumed by intention, or the people by their understanding,

89

where still there was forgiveness in time, so that whatever
had been destroyed might yet return. Around me
as I walked were dogs barking in resentment
against the coming of the unforeseen.

Finally I stood where the old sea marsh,
native to that place, had been confined below the sight
of the only-foreseeing eye. What had been the overworld
had become the underworld: the land risen from the sea
by no human intention, the drawing in and out of the water,
the pulse of the great sea now bound in a narrow ditch.

Where the Sabbath of that place kept itself in waiting,
the herons of the night stood in their morning watch,
and the herons of the day in silence stood
by the living water in its strait. The coots and gallinules
skulked in the reeds, the mother mallards and their little ones
stayed at rest upon the seaward-sliding water.
The stilts were feeding in the shallows, and the killdeer
treading with light feet the mud that was all ashine
with the coming day. Volleys of swallows leapt
in joyous flight out of the dark into the brightening air
in eternal gratitude for life before time not foreseen,
and the song of the song sparrow rang in its bush.

IV

Now Loyce Flood is dead,
A stone is at her head,
The green sod over her,
The snow will cover her.
Owen lay in that place,
The commonwealth of peace,
Fifteen years to the day
Before she came to stay.
We left them there together,
Safe now from time and weather,
At rest as man and wife.
I thank them for the life
That they in marriage made,
Faithful and unafraid,
Frugal and bountiful.
May what was beautiful
In all they said and did
Or thought and left unsaid
Flow to them like a river
And comfort them forever.

V

He thought to keep himself from Hell
By knowing and by loving well.
His work and vision, his desire
Would keep him climbing up the stair.

At limit now of flesh and bone,
He cannot climb for holding on.
"I fear the drop, I feel the blaze—
Lord, grant thy mercy and thy grace."

VI

(Andy Catlett's dream)

One morning out of time,
The final darkness passed, I wake
And rise, my body light,
Light all around. For the light's sake

I walk a narrow path
Through a steep woodland that I know,
Older and younger than
I knew, untainted by the sorrow

That I recall to find
It is not there. The light has made
A perfect greenness there,
Birdsong cascading through the shade.

Nearby there is a town
Of few houses and many graves,
Which now have filled with light.
Where love has equaled grief, who grieves?

I meet a man I've known
Always, though memory recalls
No name, a man both old
And young, dressed in clean overalls,

Who nudges his hat brim
Upward with one thumb to show me
His face. "It's Burley Coulter,
Andy. Andy, don't you know me?"

VII

(Massachusetts Avenue at Rock Creek Park, Sunday Morning)

Here by the road where people are carried, with
or against their will, as on a river of burning oil
through a time already half consumed, how
shall we pray to eacape the catastrophe
that we have not the vision to oppose and have
therefore deserved, and that many have desired?

Yet here in our moment in the ages of ages
amid the icons of fire from the maddened center
whirling out, we pray to be delivered from the blaze
that we have earned, that many desire. We pray
that the continent of love may be shaped within
the continent of power, here by the river of fire.

We pray for vision, though we die, to see
in our small imperfect love the Love of the ages
of ages, whose green tree yet stands amid the flames. May we
be as a song sung within the tree, though beside us
the river of oil flows, burning, and the sky is filled
with the whine of desire to burn and be burned in the fire.

VIII

The sky bright after summer-ending rain,
I sat against an oak half up the climb.
The sun was low; the woods was hushed in shadow;
Now the long shimmer of the crickets' song
Had stopped. I looked up to the westward ridge
And saw the ripe October light again,
Shining through leaves still green yet turning gold.
Those glowing leaves made of the light a place
That time and leaf would leave. The wind came cool,
And then I knew that I was present in
The long age of the passing world, in which
I once was not, now am, and will not be,
And in that time, beneath the changing tree,
I rested in a keeping not my own.

IX

One day I walked imagining
What work I might do here,
The place, once dark, made clear
By work and thought, my managing,
The world thus made more dear.
I walked and dreamed, the sun in clouds,
Dreamer and day at odds.

The world in its great mystery
Was hidden by my dream.
Today I make no claim;
I dream of what is here, the tree
Beside the falling stream,
The stone, the light upon the stone;
And day and dream are one.

I

The two, man and boy, wait
by their lantern, the hounds already
loose in the nearby dark.
The man calls again: "Oh, Mart!"
Soon, near the lighted window
of an invisible house beyond
the flooded creek, another light
appears, moving with the motion
of a man walking. It slants down
along the far slope, steps
onto swinging footboards
strung above the flood, crosses
slowly, swaying with the sways
of the lithe bridge, bends
around by the old road
and up the bank. Having traced
so far a man's way in this
dark world, the lantern lifts
to light the faces of the two
and of its bearer. "Yessir!
How you fellows this evenin?"

And so I came to know
The light borne in this world
By Martin Rowanberry,
Who knew no enemy,
And yet was killed by hate.
Beside the opened grave,

The hillside white with snow,
Hope makes its little song:
"And we will see him in
The morning over there."
The voices cease. And we
Can do no more for him.
The light he was returns
Unto the Light that is.

❦

Though now he has no time
For us, he stays with us
In time — a good in us
Learned from the good in him.

❦

Today the cold rain falls,
A north wind shakes the walls,
The sound earth turns to mud.
The river in brown flood
Will not return the clay
It lifts and bears away.
Now may love equal fear,
As death begins the year.

II

To give mind to machines, they are calling it
out of the world, out of the neighborhood, out of the body.
They have bound it in the brain, in the hard shell
of the skull, in order to bind it in a machine.

From the heron flying home at dusk,
from the misty hollows at sunrise,
from the stories told at the row's end,
they are calling the mind into exile
in the dry circuits of machines.

III

After the slavery of the body, dumbfoundment
of the living flesh in the order of spending
and wasting, then comes the enslavement
of consciousness, the incarnation of mind
in machines. Once the mind is reduced
to the brain, then it falls within the grasp
of the machine. It is the mind incarnate
in the body, in community, and in the earth
that they cannot confine. The difference
is love; the difference is grief and joy.
Remember the body's pleasure and its sorrow.
Remember its grief at the loss of all it knew.
Remember its redemption in suffering
and in love. Remember its resurrection
on the last day, when all made things
that have not refused this passage
will return, clarified, each fully being
in the being of all. Remember the small
secret creases of the earth—the grassy,
the wooded, the rocky—that the water
has made, finding its way. Remember
the voices of the water flowing. Remember
the water flowing under the shadows
of the trees, of the tall grasses, of the stones.
Remember the water striders walking over
the surface of the water as it flowed.
Remember the great sphere of the small
wren's song, through which the water flowed
and the light fell. Remember, and come to rest
in light's ordinary miracle.

IV

I walk in openings
That when I'm dead will close.
Where the field sparrow sings
Will come the sweet wild rose.

The yellowthroat will claim
The tangle with his song,
The redbud and wild plum
Light up the hill in spring

Where in the morning shade
My team of horses drew
The chattering iron blade,
Their fetlocks wet with dew.

Briar, bittersweet, and fern,
Box elder, locust, elm,
Cedar, wild grape, and thorn
Will reinstate the time

Of deep root and wide shadow,
Of bright, hot August calm
On the small, tree-ringed meadow
Of goldenrod and bee balm.

Thicket will grow up through
The thatches of the grass,
An old way turning new
As lives and wishes pass.

And as the thicket dies
The hickory, ash, and oak
Of the true woods will rise;
Across a long time, like

Will speak to like, the breeze
Resume old music in
The branch-ends of the trees,
The long age come again.

The hard field will find ease
In being thus released:
Let it grow wild in peace,
My workplace come to rest.

To speed this change of goods
I spare the seedling trees,
And thus invoke the woods,
The genius of this place;

I stop the mower blade,
And so conspire with time
In the return of shade,
Completion of this rhyme.

V

The body in the invisible
Familiar room accepts the gift
Of sleep, and for a while is still;
Instead of will, it lives by drift

In the great night that gathers up
The earth and sky. Slackened, unbent,
Unwanting, without fear or hope,
The body rests beyond intent.

Sleep is the prayer the body prays,
Breathing in unthought faith the Breath
That through our worry-wearied days
Preserves our rest, and is our truth.

VI

(St. Vith, December 21, 1944)

Cut off in front of the line
that now ran through St. Vith,
the five American tanks sat
in a field covered with snow
in the dark. And now they must
retreat to safety, which they
could do only through gunfire
and flame in the burning town.
They went, firing, through the fire,
GIs and German prisoners
clinging to the hulls, and out
again into the still night beyond.
In the broad dark, someone
began to sing, and one by one
the others sang also, the German
prisoners singing in German,
the Americans in English,
the one song. "Silent night,"
they sang as the great treads
passed on across the dark
countryside muffled in white
snow, "Holy night."

I

The year begins with war.
Our bombs fall day and night,
Hour after hour, by death
Abroad appeasing wrath,
Folly, and greed at home.
Upon our giddy tower
We'd oversway the world.
Our hate comes down to kill
Those whom we do not see,
For we have given up
Our sight to those in power
And to machines, and now
Are blind to all the world.
This is a nation where
No lovely thing can last.
We trample, gouge, and blast;
The people leave the land;
The land flows to the sea.
Fine men and women die,
The fine old houses fall,
The fine old trees come down:
Highway and shopping mall
Still guarantee the right
And liberty to be
A peaceful murderer,
A murderous worshipper,
A slender glutton, or
A healthy whore. Forgiving

No enemy, forgiven
By none, we live the death
Of liberty, become
What we have feared to be.

II

The ewes crowd to the mangers;
Their bellies widen, sag;
Their udders tighten. Soon
The little voices cry
In morning cold. Soon now
The garden must be worked,
Laid off in rows, the seed
Of life to come brought down
Into the dark to rest,
Abide a while alone,
And rise. Soon, soon again
The cropland must be plowed,
For the year's promise now
Answers the year's desire,
Its hunger and its hope.
This goes against the time
When food is bought, not grown
O come into the market
With cash, and come to rest
In this economy
Where all we need is money
To be well-stuffed and free
By sufferance of our Lord,
The Chairman of the Board.
Because there's thus no need,
There is the greatest need
To plant one's ground with seed.
Under the season's sway,
Against the best advice,
In time of death and tears,
In slow snowfall of years,
Defiant and in hope,
We keep an older way
In light and breath to stay
This household on its slope.

III

Now with its thunder spring
Returns. The river, raised,
Carries the rain away.
Carp wallow in the shoals
Above our flooded fields.
Jonquils return to dooryards
Of vanished houses. Phoebes
Return to build again
Under the stilted porch.
On thicketed hillsides
The young trees bud and bloom;
They stand in poisoned air
In their community.
Twinleaf and bloodroot flower
Out of the fallen leaves.
At flood's edge all night long
The little frogs are singing.
In the dark barn, hard rain
Loud on the roof, long time
Till dawn, the young ewe calls
The lamb yet in her womb.

IV

The team rests in shade at the edge
of the half-harrowed field, the first
warm morning of May. Wind breathes
over the worked ground, through maples
by the creek, moving every new leaf.
The stream sings quietly in passing.
Too late for frost, too early for flies,
the air carries only birdsong, the long
draft of wind through leaves. In this time
I could stay forever. In my wish
to stay forever, it stays forever.
But I must go. Mortal and obliged,
I shake off stillness, stand, and go back
to the waiting field, unending rounds.

V

The seed is in the ground.
Now may we rest in hope
While darkness does its work.

VI   THE LOCUSTS

Seventeen more years, and they are here
again, having risen up out of the dark,
emerged winged out of their riven shells
to fly in light, to mate and die,
and yet again return, in God's economy
that lets no made thing finally fall.
And we, who vowed ourselves to one another
twice seventeen years ago, know like these
the hard patience of being dark, separate,
and half alive. Like them, from time
to time we rise up, become full grown,
complex, and whole. Become one,
the true person we are pledged to be,
we leave the dark. Mortal and destined,
earthen and winged, we come into the light.

VII

Where the great trees were felled
The thorns and thistles grow
From the unshaded ground,
And so the Fall's renewed
And all the creatures mourn,
Groan and travail in pain
Together until now.
And yet their Maker's here,
Within and over all
Now and forevermore,
Being and yet to be
In columbine, oak tree,
Woodthrush, beetle, and worm,
In song of thrush and stream,
Fact, mystery, and dream:
Spirit in love with form,
And loving to inform
Form formed within itself
As thought, fulfilled in flesh,
And made to live by breath
Breathed into it by love.
The violence past for now,
The felling and the falling
Done, as a mourner walks
Restless from room to room,
I cross the stream to find
On a neglected slope
The woods' floor starred with bloom.

VIII

What do the tall trees say
To the late havocs in the sky?
They sigh.
The air moves, and they sway.
When the breeze on the hill
Is still, then they stand still.
They wait.
They have no fear. Their fate
Is faith. Birdsong
Is all they've wanted, all along.

IX THE FARM

Go by the narrow road
Along the creek, a burrow
Under shadowy trees
Such as a mouse makes through
Tall grass, so that you may
Forget the wide road you
Have left behind, and all
That it has led to. Or,
Best, walk up through the woods,
Around the valley rim,
And down to where the trees
Give way to cleared hillside,
So that you reach the place
Out of the trees' remembrance
Of their kind; seasonal
And timeless, they stand in
Uncounted time, and you
Have passed among them, small
As a mouse at a feast,
Unnoticed at the feet
Of all those mighty guests.
Come on a clear June morning
As the fog lifts, trees drip,
And birds make everywhere
Uninterrupted song.

However you may come,
You'll see it suddenly
Lie open to the light
Amid the woods: a farm
Little enough to see
Or call across—cornfield,
Hayfield, and pasture, clear

As if remembered, dreamed
And yearned for long ago,
Neat as a blossom now
With all the pastures mowed
And the dew fresh upon it,
Bird music all around.
That is the vision, seen
As on a Sabbath walk:
The possibility
Of human life whose terms
Are Heaven's and this earth's.

Stay years if you would know
The work and thought, the pleasure
And grief, the feat, by which
This vision lives. In fall
Or winter you should plow
A patch of bottomland
For corn; the freezes then
Will work the heavy clods.
When it's too wet to plow,
Go to the woods to fell
Trees for next winter's fuel.
Take the inferior trees
And not all from one place,
So that the woods will yield
Without diminishment.
Then trim and rick the logs;
And when you drag them out
From woods to rick, use horses
Whose hooves are kinder to
The ground than wheels. In spring
The traces of your work
Will be invisible.

Near winter's end, your flock
Will bear their lambs, and you
Must be alert, out late
And early at the barn,
To guard against the grief
You cannot help but feel
When any young thing made
For life falters at birth
And dies. Save the best hay
To feed the suckling ewes.
Shelter them in the barn
Until the grass is strong,
Then turn them out to graze
The green hillsides, good pasture
With shade and water close.
Then watch for dogs, whose sport
Will be to kill your sheep
And ruin all your work.
Or old Coyote may
Become your supper guest,
Unasked and without thanks;
He'll just excerpt a lamb
And dine before you know it.
But don't, because of that,
Make war against the world
And its wild appetites.
A guard dog or a jenny
Would be the proper answer;
Or use electric fence.
For you must learn to live
With neighbors never chosen
As with the ones you chose.
Coyote's song at midnight
Says something for the world
The world wants said. And when
You know your flock is safe

You'll like to wake and hear
That wild voice sing itself
Free in the dark, at home.

As the fields dry, complete
Your plowing; you must do this
As early as you can.
Then disk and drag the furrows.
And now the past must come
To serve the future: dung
And straw from the barn floor
You carry to the fields,
Load after load until
The barns are clean, the cropland
All covered with manure.
In early May, prepare
The corn ground, plant the corn.
And now you are committed.
Wait for the seed to sprout,
The green shoots, lightly rolled,
To show above the ground
As risen from the grave.
Then you must cultivate
To keep them free of weeds
Until they have grown tall
And can defend themselves.

Where you grew corn last year,
Sow buckwheat, let it seed,
Then disk it in and grow
A second crop to disk in.
This is for humus, and
To keep out weeds. It is
A Sabbath for the land,
Rest and enrichment, good
For it, for you, for all

The ones who are unborn;
The land must have its Sabbath
Or take it when we starve.
The ground is mellow now,
Friable and porous: rich.
Mid-August is the time
To sow this field in clover
And grass, to cut for hay
Two years, pasture a while,
And then return to corn.

But don't neglect your garden.
Household economy
Makes family and land
An independent state.
Never buy at a store
What you can grow or find
At home — this is the rule
Of liberty, also
Of neighborhood. (And be
Faithful to local merchants
Too. Never buy far off
What you can buy near home.)
As early as you can,
Plant peas, onions, and greens,
Potatoes, radishes,
Cabbage and cauliflower,
Lettuce, carrots, and beets —
Things that will stand the frost.
Then as the weather warms
Plant squashes, corn, and beans,
Okra, tomatoes, herbs,
Flowers — some for yourself
And some to give away.
In the cornfield plant pole beans,

Pumpkins, and winter squash;
Thus by diversity
You can enlarge the yield.

You have good grass and hay,
So keep a cow or two.
Milk made from your own grass
Is cheap and sweet. A cow
To milk's a good excuse
To bring you home from places
You do not want to be.
Fatten the annual calf
For slaughter. Keep a pig
To rescue scraps, skimmed milk,
And other surpluses.
Keep hens who will make eggs
And meat of offal, insects,
A little of your corn.
Eat these good beasts that eat
What you can't eat. Be thankful
To them and to the plants,
To your small, fertile homeland,
To topsoil, light, and rain
That daily give you life.

Be thankful and repay
Growth with good work and care.
Work done in gratitude,
Kindly, and well is prayer.
You did not make yourself,
Yet you must keep yourself
By use of other lives.
No gratitude atones
For bad use or too much.

This is not work for hire.
By this expenditure
You make yourself a place;
You make yourself a way
For love to reach the ground.
In its ambition and
Its greed, its violence,
The world is turned against
This possibility,
And yet the world survives
By the survival of
This kindly working love.

And while you work your fields
Do not forget the woods.
The woods stands by the field
To measure it, and teach
Its keeper. Nature is
The best farmer, for she
Preserves the land, conserves
The rain; she deepens soil,
Wastes nothing; and she is
Diverse and orderly.
She is our mother, teacher,
And final judge on earth.
The farm's a human order
Opening among the trees,
Remembering the woods.
To farm, live like a tree
That does not grow beyond
The power of its place.
It rises by the strength
Of local soil and light,
Aspiring to no height
That it has not attained.
More time, more light, more rain

Will make it grow again
Till it has realized
All that it can become,
And then it dies into
More life, deserving more
By not desiring more.

The year's first fullness comes
To the hayfields. In May,
Watching the sky, you mow
Your fields before the grass
Toughens and while the clover
Stands in its early bloom.
But weather's iffy here
In May, and in these close
Valleys, the early cutting
Is hard to cure. Some rain
Will fall on swath or windrow,
As like as not, to darken
The hay. It beats a snowball,"
You say then to console
Yourself, and look ahead
To later cuttings, lighter,
Better, quicker to dry.
In summer, thus, you think
Of winter, load the barns
In heat against the cold,
The January days
When you'll go out to feed,
Your breath a little cloud,
The blue air glittery
With frost. On the tracked snow,
On ground that's frozen hard,
You free the smell of summer
From bales of hay thrown down
Before the hungry stock.

Soon you have salad greens
Out of the garden rows,
Then peas, early potatoes,
Onions, beets, beans, sweet corn.
The bounty of the year
Now comes in like a tide:
Yellow summer squashes,
Pole beans from the cornfield,
Tomatoes, okra, eggplant,
Cabbage and cauliflower.
Eat, and give to the neighbors;
Preserve for wintertime;
Plant more, and fight the weeds.
Later will come the fall crops:
Turnips, parsnips, more greens,
The winter squashes, cushaws,
And pumpkins big as tubs.
"Too much for us," you'll say,
And give some more away.
Or try to; nowadays,
A lot of people would
Rather work hard to buy
Their food already cooked
Than get it free by work.

Best of all is the fruit,
Sweetest and prettiest:
The strawberries and cherries,
The gooseberries and currants,
Raspberries and blackberries
(The best are wild), grapes, pears,
Apples early and late—
These gleamings in the sun
That gleam upon the tongue
And gleam put up in jars
And gleam within the mind.

Of all your harvests, those
Are pleasantest that come
Freest: blackberries from
Wild fencerows; strawberries
You happen on in crossing
The grassy slopes in June;
Wild cherries and wild grapes,
Sour at first taste, then sweet;
Persimmons and blackhaws
That you gather and eat
On days you walk among
The red and yellow leaves;
And walnuts, hickory nuts
Gathered beneath the trees.
In your wild foragings
The earth feeds you the way
She feeds the beasts and birds.

And all the summer long
You're putting up more hay,
You clip the pastures, keep
The fences up, repair
Your buildings, milk your cows;
You wean the lambs; you move
The livestock to new grass;
And you must walk the fields
With hoe in hand, to cut
The thistles and the docks.
There is no end to work—
Work done in pleasure, grief,
Or weariness, with ease
Of skill and timeliness,
Or awkwardly or wrong,
Too hurried or too slow.
One job completed shows
Another to be done.

And so you make the farm
That must be daily made
And yearly made, or it
Will not exist. If you
Should go and not return
And none should follow you,
This clarity would be
As if it never was.
But praise, in knowing this,
The Genius of the place,
Whose ways forgive your own
And will resume again
In time, if left alone.
You work always in this
Dear opening between
What was and is to be.

And so you make the farm,
And so you disappear
Into your days, your days
Into the ground. Before
You start each day, the place
Is as it is, and at
The day's end, it is as
It is, a little changed
By work, but still itself,
Having included you
And everything you've done.
And it is who you are,
And you are what it is.
You will work many days
No one will ever see;
Their record is the place.
This way you come to know
That something moves in time
That time does not contain.

For by this timely work
You keep yourself alive
As you came into time,
And as you'll leave: God's dust,
God's breath, a little Light.

To rest, go to the woods
Where what is made is made
Without your thought or work.
Sit down; begin the wait
For small trees to grow big,
Feeding on earth and light.
Their good result is song
The winds must bring, that trees
Must wait to sing, and sing
Longer than you can wait.
Soon you must go. The trees,
Your seniors, standing thus
Acknowledged in your eyes,
Stand as your praise and prayer.
Your rest is in this praise
Of what you cannot be
And what you cannot do.

But make your land recall,
In workdays of the fields,
The Sabbath of the woods.
Although your fields must bear
The barbed seed of the Fall,
Though nations yet make war
For madness and for hire,
By work in harmony
With the God-given world
You bring your days to rest,
Remain a living soul.
In time of hate and waste,

Wars and rumors of wars,
Rich armies and poor peace,
Your blessed economy,
Beloved sufficiency
Upon a dear, small place,
Sings with the morning stars.

Autumn ripens the corn.
You pick the yellow ears,
Carry them from the field,
Rich, satisfying loads.
The garden's final yield
Now harvested, the ground
Worked and manured, prepared
For spring, put out of mind,
You must saw, split, bring in,
And store your winter wood.
And thus the year comes round.

X

Loving you has taught me the infinite
longing of the self to be given away
and the great difficulty of that entire
giving, for in love to give is to receive
and then there is yet more to give;
and others have been born of our giving
to whom the self, greatened by gifts,
must be given, and by that giving
be increased, until, self-burdened,
the self, staggering upward in years,
in fear, hope, love, and sorrow,
imagines, rising like a moon,
a pale moon risen in daylight
over the dark woods, the Self
whose gift we and all others are,
the self that is by definition given.

I

The winter world of loss
And grief is gone. The night
Is past. Along the whole
Length of the river, birds
Are singing in the trees.

Again, hope dreams itself
Awake. The year's first lambs
Cry in the morning dark.
And, after all, we have
A garden in our minds.

We living know the worth
Of all the dead have done
Or hoped to do. We know
That hearts, against their doom,
Must plight an ancient troth.

Now come the bride and groom,
Now come the man and woman
Who must begin again
The work divine and human
By which we live on earth.

(Pryor Clifford & Billie Carol – March 7, 1992)

II

Lift up the dead leaves
and see, waiting
in the dark, in cold March,

the purplish stems, leaves,
and buds of twinleaf,
infinitely tender, infinitely

expectant. They straighten
slowly into the light after
the nights of frost. At last

the venture is made: the brief
blossoms open, the petals fall,
the hinged capsules of seed

grow big. The possibility
of this return returns
again to the seed, the dark,

the long wait, and the light again.

III

Again we come
to the resurrection
of bloodroot from the dark,

a hand that reaches up
out of the ground,
holding a lamp.

IV

I went away only
a few hundred steps
up the hill, and turned
and started home.
And then I saw
the pasture green under
the trees, the open
hillside, the little ponds,
our house, cistern,
woodshed, and barn,
the river bending in
its valley, our garden
new-planted beside it.
All around, the woods
that had been stark
in the harsh air
of March, had turned
soft with new leaves.
Birdsong had returned
to the branches:
the stream sang
in the fold of the hill.
In its time and its patience
beauty had come upon us,
greater than I had imagined.

V

I too am not at home
When you are gone
And I am here alone.
Until you come

I am as dead, condemned
To fractionhood,
A stillness of the blood,
Dark in the ground.

But I rise up alive
When you come near
Our place of flowers where
Alone I live.

VI

My sore ran in the night
and ceased not. I tossed to and fro
unto the dawning of the day.
Let the sighs of the prisoner
come before thee; according to
the greatness of thy power
preserve thou those that are
appointed to die. I remembered
my song in the night. I said,
This is my sorrow, but I will
remember the works of the Lord;
I will remember his wonders
of old. And I remembered
the small stream coming down
off the hill through all the years
of my people, and long before.
I remembered the trees on the slopes
beside it, standing in the great heat
of summer, and giving shade.
I remembered the leaves falling
and then the snow, and again
the small flowers rising up
out of dead leaves, the mosses
green again by the flowing water,
and the water thrush's nest
under the root of a strong tree.
I said, I will grieve no more
for death, for what is death to me
who have seen thy returns, O
Lord of love, who in the false are true.

VII

Those who give their thought
to seed, to love and the bringing to birth,
must know the sightless underside
of earth, and perhaps more than once,
for no one goes at no cost
to that place where what is dark,
more still than the hands
of the dead, remembers the light
again, and starts to move.

It is spring, and the little trees
that sprouted in the abandoned field
two years and more ago, striving
to grow, half-smothered under
the shadows of the tall weeds,
now rise above them
and spread their newleafed branches,
nothing between them and the light
sky, nothing at all.

VIII

I have again come home
through miles of sky
from hours of abstract talk
in the way of modern times
when humans live in their minds
and the world, forgotten, dies
into explanations. Weary
with absence, I return to earth.
"Good to see you back down
on the creek!" Martin Rowanberry
would say if he were here
to say it, as he'll not be again.
I have departed and returned
too many times to forget
that after all returns
one departure will remain.
I bring the horses down
off the hillside, harness them,
and start the morning's work,
the team quick to the load
along the narrow road.
I am weary with days
of travel, with poor sleep,
with time and error,
with every summer's heat
and blood-drinking flies.
And yet I sink into
the ancient happiness
of slow work in unhastenable
days and years. Horse and cow,
plow and hoe, grass to graze
and hay to mow have brought me
here, and taught me where I am.
I work in absence not yet mine

that will be mine. In time
this place has come to signify
the absence of many, and always
more, who once were here.
Day by day their voices
come to me, as from the air.
I remember them in what I do.
So I am not a modern man.
In my work I would be known
by forebears of a thousand years
if they were here to see it.
So it has been. So be it.

IX THIRTY-FIVE YEARS

We have kept to the way we chose
in love without foresight
and long ago; it has come
to light only in the daylight
of each day as that day has come—
out of many possibilities, one:
an old house renewed upon its slope;
a long bringing in from garden,
field, and woods, not to be
hurried or increased beyond
the power of the place and day;
hope and grief freely given
to the unborn, the young, the old,
and the dead in their berths
under their silent names.
We have kept a daily faithfulness
to these, to one another, and to
this difficult, beautiful place,
arriving here again and again
out of distance, weariness,
or disappointment, to take it
by surprise, our surprise,
as the newborn take, after long
sightlessness, the light of day.
It is an old road that we
have followed, too narrow
to be traveled by more than two,
affording no place to turn
and go back, little improved
by the passage of forebears,
yet always renewed by growth
of the trees that lean over it,
by weather never two days the same,
and by our own delight

to see that it has led us
once again to an opening,
a small cultivated valley
among the wooded hills, familiar
as the oldest dream, where we know
we are, even as we do,
the work of love.

I

No, no, there is no going back.
Less and less you are
that possibility you were.
More and more you have become
those lives and deaths
that have belonged to you.
You have become a sort of grave
containing much that was
and is no more in time, beloved
then, now, and always.
And you have become a sort of tree
standing over a grave.
Now more than ever you can be
gracious toward each day
that comes, young, to disappear
forever, and yet remain
unaging in the mind.
Every day you have less reason
not to give yourself away.

II

When my father was an old man,
past eighty years, we sat together
on the porch in silence
in the dark. Finally he said,
"Well, I have had a wonderful life,"
adding after a long pause,
"and I have had nothing
to do with it!" We were silent
for a while again. And then I asked,
"Well, do you believe in the
'informed decision'?" He thought
some more, and at last said
out of the darkness: "Naw!"
He was right, for when we choose
the way by which our only life
is lived, we choose and do not know
what we have chosen, for this
is the heart's choice, not the mind's;
to be true to the heart's one choice
is the long labor of the mind.
He chose, imperfectly as we must,
the rule of love, and learned
through years of light what darkly
he had chosen: his life, his place,
our place, our lives. And now comes
one he chose, but will not see:
Emily Rose, born May 2, 1993.

III

Now, surely, I am getting old,
for my memory of myself
as a young man seems now
to be complete, as a story told.
The young man leaps, and lands
on an old man's legs.

IV

Hate has no world.
The people of hate must try
to possess the world of love,
for it is the only world;
it is Heaven and Earth.
But as lonely, eager hate
possesses it, it disappears;
it never did exist,
and hate must seek another
world that love has made.

V   REMEMBERING EVIA

For Liadain, Denise, and Philip Sherrard

We went in darkness where
We did not know, or why
Or how we'd come so far
Past sight or memory.

We climbed a narrow path
Up a moon-shadowed slope.
The guide we journeyed with
Held a small light. And step

By step our shadows rose
With us, and then fell back
Before the shine of windows
That opened in the black

Hillside, or so it seemed.
We reached a windy porch
As if both seen and dreamed
On its dark, lofty perch

Between the sky and sea.
A lamplit table spread
Old hospitality
Of cheese and wine and bread.

Darker than wine, the waves
Muttered upon the stones,
Asking whose time it was,
Our time or Agamemnon's.

The sea's undying sound
Demarked a land unknown
To us, who therein found
Welcome, our travel done.

I

In Memory: William Stafford

I leave the warmth of the stove,
my chair and book, and go out
into the cold night. My little lamp
that shows the way and leaves me dark
is swinging in my hand.
The house windows shine above me,
and below a single light gleams
in the barn where an hour ago
I left a ewe in labor. Beyond
is the grand sweep of Heaven's stars.
As I walk between them in the deep
night, the lights of house and barn
also are stars; my own small light
is an unsteady star.
I come to earth on the barn floor
where the ewe's lambs have been born
and now, wet and bloody, breathing
at last the air of this wintry world,
struggle to rise, while the ewe
mutters and licks. Unknowing,
they have the knack of their becoming:
heartbeat and breath,
the hunger that will lead them
to the tit, and thence to the sunlit
grass. I perform the ancient acts
of comfort and safety, making sure.
I linger a moment in the pleasure
of their coming and my welcome,

and then go, for I must comfort myself
and sleep. While I worked
the world turned half an hour,
carrying us on toward morning
and spring, the dark and the cold
again, the births and then the deaths
of many things, the end of time.
I close the door and walk back,
homeward, among the stars.

II

Finally will it not be enough,
after much living, after
much love, after much dying
of those you have loved,
to sit on the porch near sundown
with your eyes simply open,
watching the wind shape the clouds
into the shapes of clouds?

Even then you will remember
the history of love, shaped
in the shapes of flesh, everchanging
as the clouds that pass, the blessed
yearning of body for body,
unending light.
You will remember, watching
the clouds, the future of love.

III

(Ye must be born again.)

I think of Gloucester, blind, led through the world
To the world's edge by the hand of a stranger
Who is his faithful son. At the cliff's verge
He flings away his life, as of no worth,
The true way lost, his eyes two bleeding wounds—
And finds his life again, and is led on
By the forsaken son who has become
His father, that the good may recognize
Each other, and at last go ripe to death.
We live the given life, and not the planned.

IV

They sit together on the porch, the dark
Almost fallen, the house behind them dark.
Their supper done with, they have washed and dried
The dishes—only two plates now, two glasses,
Two knives, two forks, two spoons—small work for two.
She sits with her hands folded in her lap,
At rest. He smokes his pipe. They do not speak.
And when they speak at last it is to say
What each one knows the other knows. They have
One mind between them, now, that finally
For all its knowing will not exactly know
Which one goes first through the dark doorway, bidding
Goodnight, and which sits on a while alone.

V

For Maxine Kumin

Raking hay on a rough slope,
when I was about sixteen,
I drove to the ridgetop and saw
in a neighbor's field on the other side
a pond in a swale, and around it
the whole field filled
with chicory in bloom, blue
as the sky reflected in the pond—
bluer even, and somehow lighter,
though they belonged to gravity.
They were the morning's
blossoms and would not last.
But I go back now in my mind
to when I drew the long windrow
to the top of the rise, and I see
the blue-flowered field, holding
in its center the sky-reflecting pond.
It seems, as then, another world
in this world, such as a pilgrim
might travel days and years
to find, and find at last
on the morning of his return
by his mere being at home
awake—a moment seen, forever known.

VI

A man is lying on a bed
in a small room in the dark.
Weary and afraid, he prays
for courage to sleep, to wake
and work again; he doubts
that waking when he wakes
will recompense his sleep.
His prayers lean upward
on the dark and fall
like flares from a catastrophe.
He is a man breathing the fear
of hopeless prayer, prayed
in hope. He breathes the prayer
of his fear that gives a light
by which he sees only himself lying
in the dark, a low mound asking
almost nothing at all.
And then, long yet before dawn,
comes what he had not thought:
love that causes him to stir
like the dead in the grave, being
remembered—his own love or
Heaven's, he does not know.
But now it is all around him;
it comes down upon him
like a summer rain falling
slowly, quietly in the dark.

VII

I would not have been a poet
except that I have been in love
alive in this mortal world,
or an essayist except that I
have been bewildered and afraid,
or a storyteller had I not heard
stories passing to me through the air,
or a writer at all except
I have been wakeful at night
and words have come to me
out of their deep caves,
needing to be remembered.
But on the days I am lucky
or blessed, I am silent.
I go into the one body
that two make in making marriage
that for all our trying, all
our deaf-and-dumb of speech,
has no tongue. Or I give myself
to gravity, light, and air
and am carried back
to solitary work in fields
and woods, where my hands
rest upon a world unnamed,
complete, unanswerable, and final
as our daily bread and meat.
The way of love leads all ways
to life beyond words, silent
and secret. To serve that triumph
I have done all the rest.

VIII

And now this leaf lies brightly on the ground.

I

A man with some authentic worries
And many vain and silly ones,
I am well-schooled in sleeplessness;
I know it from the inside out.
I breathe, and I know what's at stake.

But still sometimes I'm sane and sound,
However heart or head may ache;
I go to sleep when I lie down.
With no determined care to breathe,
I breathe and live and sleep and take

A sabbath from my worrying.
I rest in an unasking trust
Like clouds and ponds and stones and trees.
The long-arising Day will break
If I should die before I wake.

II

The best reward in going to the woods
Is being lost to other people, and
Lost sometimes to myself. I'm at the end
Of no bespeaking wire to spoil my goods;

I send no letter back I do not bring.
Whoever wants me now must hunt me down
Like something wild, and wild is anything
Beyond the reach of purpose not its own.

Wild is anything that's not at home
In something else's place. This good white oak
Is not an orchard tree, is unbespoke,
And it can live here by its will alone,

Lost to all other wills but Heaven's—wild.
So where I most am found I'm lost to you,
Presuming friend, and only can be called
Or answered by a certain one, or two.

III   A BRASS BOWL

Worn to brightness, this
bowl opens outward
to the world, like
the marriage of a pair
we sometimes know.
Filled full, it holds
not greedily. Empty,
it fills with light
that is Heaven's and
its own. It holds
forever for a while.

IV   AMISH ECONOMY

We live by mercy if we live.
To that we have no fit reply
But working well and giving thanks,
Loving God, loving one another,
To keep Creation's neighborhood.

And my friend David Kline told me,
"It falls strangely on Amish ears,
This talk of how you find yourself.
We Amish, after all, don't try
To find ourselves. We try to lose
Ourselves"—and thus are lost within
The found world of sunlight and rain
Where fields are green and then are ripe,
And the people eat together by
The charity of God, who is kind
Even to those who give no thanks.

In morning light, men in dark clothes
Go out among the beasts and fields.
Lest the community be lost,
Each day they must work out the bond
Between goods and their price: the garden
Weeded by sweat is flowerbright;
The wheat shocked in shorn fields, clover
Is growing where wheat grew; the crib
Is golden with the gathered corn,

While in the world of the found selves,
Lost to the sunlit, rainy world,
The motor-driven cannot stop.
This is the world where value is
Abstract, and preys on things, and things
Are changed to thoughts that have a price.

Cost + greed − fear = price:
Maury Telleen thus laid it out.
The need to balance greed and fear
Affords no stopping place, no rest,
And need increases as we fail.

But now, in summer dusk, a man
Whose hair and beard curl like spring ferns
Sits under the yard trees, at rest,
His smallest daughter on his lap.
This is because he rose at dawn,
Cared for his own, helped his neighbors,
Worked much, spent little, kept his peace.

V

To my granddaughters who visited the Holocaust
Museum on the day of the burial of Yitzhak Rabin

Now you know the worst
we humans have to know
about ourselves, and I am sorry,

for I know that you will be afraid.
To those of our bodies given
without pity to be burned, I know

there is no answer
but loving one another,
even our enemies, and this is hard.

But remember:
when a man of war becomes a man of peace,
he gives a light, divine

though it is also human.
When a man of peace is killed
by a man of war, he gives a light.

You do not have to walk in darkness.
If you will have the courage for love,
you may walk in light. It will be

the light of those who have suffered
for peace. It will be
your light.

VI · THE OLD MAN CLIMBS A TREE

He had a tall cedar he wanted to cut for posts,
but it leaned backward toward the fence,
and there's no gain in tearing down one
fence to build another. To preserve the fence
already built, he needed to fasten a rope
high up in the cedar, and draw it tight
to the trunk of another tree, so that as he sawed
the cedar free of its stance it would sway
away from the fence as it fell. To bring
a ladder would require too long a carry
up through the woods. Besides, you can't
climb into a cedar tree by means of a ladder —
too branchy. He would need first to cut off
all the branches, and for that would need a ladder.

And so, he thought, he would need to climb
the tree itself. He'd climbed trees many times
in play when he was a boy, and many times
since, when he'd had a reason. He'd loved
always his reasons for climbing trees.
But he'd come now to the age of remembering,
and he remembered his boyhood fall from an apple tree,
and being brought in to his mother, his wits
dispersed, not knowing where he was,
though where he was was this world still.
If that should happen now, he thought,
the world he waked up in would not be this one.
The other world is nearer to him now.
But trailing his rope untied as yet to anything
but himself, he climbed up once again and stood
where only birds and the wind had been before,
and knew it was another world, after all,
that he had climbed up into. There are
no worlds but other worlds: the world

of the field mouse, the world of the hawk,
the world of the beetle, the world of the oak,
the worlds of the unborn, the dead, and all
the heavenly host, and he is alive
in those worlds while living in his own.
Known or unknown, every world exists
because the others do.

        The treetops
are another world, smelling of bark,
a stratum of freer air and larger views,
from which he saw the world he'd lived in
all day until now, its intimate geography changed
by his absence and by the height he saw it from.
The sky was a little larger, and all around
the aerial topography of treetops, green and gray,
the ground almost invisible beneath.
He perched there, ungravitied as a bird,
knotting his rope and looking about, worlded
in worlds on worlds, pleased, and unafraid.

There are no worlds but other worlds
and all the other worlds are here,
reached or almost reachable by the same
outstretching hand, as he, perched upon
his high branch, almost imagined flight.
And yet when he descended into this other
other world, he climbed down all the way.
He did not swing out from a lower limb
and drop, as once he would have done.

✿✿✿✿✿✿✿✿✿✿✿ 1996 ✿✿✿✿✿✿✿✿✿✿✿

I

In Memory: Jane Kenyon

Now you have slipped away
Under the trackless snow,
To you the time of day
Always is long ago.

You're safe among the dead,
Alive, your death undone.
"Come and dine," Christ said.
Consenting, you have gone.

II

On summer evenings we sat in the yard,
the house dark, the stars bright overhead.
The laps and arms of the old
held the young. As we talked we knew
by the dark distances of Heaven's lights
our smallness, and the greatness of our love.

Now from that upland once surrounded
by the horizon of unbroken dark, we
(who were children only a life ago)
see reflected on the clouds the lights
of three cities, as if we offer to the sky
some truth of ours that we are certain of,

as if we will have no light
but our own, and thus make illusory
all the light we have.

III

In Memory: Morgan Perry

It is almost spring again.
At the woods' edge the redbird
sings his happiest note: sweet,
sweet, sweet, sweet. And you,
who have left this world forever,
have been gone one day.

March 15, 1996

IV

A long time ago, returning
from a trip to see a girl
with whom I was in love,
I stopped on the roadside
above this house where I now live.
I had driven all day and on
into the night. Now it was late.
Moonlight covered the world,
and the valley was filled
with voices, the whippoorwills
calling and answering
in the hollows and along the slopes,
so that their music seemed
to gather and flow as the moonlight
flowed and touched lightly
every upward leaf and grassblade.
I stood still a long time for fear
that any sound I made
would cause that flood of light,
which was singing which was
light, to flow away forever
from this flawed world. I forgot
the misery of a boy's love
inevitably selfish, and a selfless
happiness freely came to me
from this place, to which my heart
for longer had been given.

V

Some Sunday afternoon, it may be,
you are sitting under your porch roof,
looking down through the trees
to the river, watching the rain. The circles
made by the raindrops' striking
expand, intersect, dissolve,

and suddenly (for you are getting on
now, and much of your life is memory)
the hands of the dead, who have been here
with you, rest upon you tenderly
as the rain rests shining
upon the leaves. And you think then

(for thought will come) of the strangeness
of the thought of Heaven, for now
you have imagined yourself there,
remembering with longing this
happiness, this rain. Sometimes here
we are there, and there is no death.

VI

A bird the size
of a leaf fills
the whole lucid
evening with
his note, and flies.

VII

In spring we planted seed,
And by degrees the plants
Grew, flowered, and transformed
The light to food, which we
Brought in, and ate, and lived.
The year grown old, we gathered
All that remained. We broke,
Manured, prepared the ground
For overwintering,
And thus at last made clear
Our little plot of time,
Tropical for a while,
Then temperate, then cold.

VIII

Our Christmas tree is
not electrified, is not
covered with little lights
calling attention to themselves
(we have had enough
of little lights calling attention
to themselves). Our tree
is a cedar cut here, one
of the fragrances of our place,
hung with painted cones
and paper stars folded
long ago to praise our tree,
Christ come into the world.

I

Best of any song
is bird song
in the quiet, but first
you must have the quiet.

II

Even while I dreamed I prayed that what I saw was only fear
        and no foretelling,
for I saw the last known landscape destroyed for the sake
of the objective, the soil bulldozed, the rock blasted.
Those who had wanted to go home would never get there
        now.

I visited the offices where for the sake of the objective the
        planners planned
at blank desks set in rows. I visited the loud factories
where the machines were made that would drive ever
        forward
toward the objective. I saw the forest reduced to stumps and
        gullies; I saw
the poisoned river, the mountain cast into the valley;
I came to the city that nobody recognized because it looked
        like every other city.
I saw the passages worn by the unnumbered
footfalls of those whose eyes were fixed upon the objective.

Their passage had obliterated the graves and the
        monuments
of those who had died in pursuit of the objective
and who had long ago forever been forgotten, according
to the invariable rule that those who have forgotten forget
that they have forgotten. Men and women and children now
        pursued the objective
as if nobody ever had pursued it before.

The races and the sexes now intermingled perfectly in
        pursuit of the objective.
The once-enslaved, the once-oppressed were now free
to sell themselves to the highest bidder
and to enter the best-paying prisons

in pursuit of the objective, which was the destruction of all
      enemies,
which was the destruction of all obstacles, which was to clear
      the way
to victory which was to clear the way to promotion, to
      salvation, to progress,
to the completed sale, to the signature
on the contract, which was to clear the way
to self-realization, to self-creation, from which nobody who
      ever wanted to go home
would ever get there now, for every remembered place
had been displaced; the signposts had been bent to the
      ground and covered over.

Every place had been displaced, every love
unloved, every vow unsworn, every work unmeant
to make way for the passage of the crowd
of the individuated, the autonomous, the self-actuated,
      the homeless
with their many eyes opened only toward the objective
which they did not yet perceive in the far distance,
having never known where they were going,
having never known where they came from.

III

I was wakened from my dream of the ruined world by the sound
of rain falling slowly onto the dry earth of my place in time.
On the parched garden, the cracked-open pastures,
the dusty grape leaves, the brittled grass, the drooping foilage of
        the woods,
fell still the quiet rain.

IV

"You see," my mother said, and laughed,
knowing I knew the passage
she was remembering, "finally you lose
everything." She had lost
parents, husband, friends, youth,
health, most comforts, many hopes.

Deaf, asleep in her chair, awakened
by a hand's touch, she would look up
and smile in welcome as quiet
as if she had seen us coming.

She watched, curious and affectionate,
the sparrows, titmice, and chickadees
she fed at her kitchen window—
where did they come from, where
did they go? No matter.
They came and went as freely as
in the time of her old age
her children came and went,
uncaptured, but fed.

And I, walking in the first spring
of her absence, know again
her inextinguishable delight:
the wild bluebells, the yellow
celandine, violets purple
and white, twinleaf, bloodroot,
larkspur, the rue anemone
light, light under the big trees,
and overhead the redbud blooming,
the redbird singing,
the oak leaves like flowers still
unfolding, and the blue sky.

V

The lovers know the loveliness
That is not of their bodies only
(Though they be lovely) but is of
Their bodies given up to love.

They find the open-heartedness
Of two desires which both are lonely
Until by dying they have their living,
And gain all they have lost in giving,

Each offering the desired desire.
Beyond what time requires, they are
What they surpass themselves to make;
They give the pleasure that they take.

VI

Now, as a man learning
the limits of time, I look anew
at a familiar carving: a ring
of granite drawing to a circle

all space around it, and enclosing
a circle. In cross section, the stone
itself is square. It doubles
the superficial strip of Möbius

and thus makes of two surfaces
a solid, dimensioned
as the body, a pure thought
shaped in stone. One surface

is rough, the other smooth,
to invite hand or eye into
its windings, to remind the mind
in its travels, the long and far

of its restless reckoning,
that where it comes from
and where it is going
are nowhere in the distance,

not in the future or the past,
but are forever here
now. The stone turns
without limit within itself,

dark within light, light
within dark. What is above
descends, what is below rises.
So the carver wrought it out

179

until it came to rest.
So what is inward turns outward
as does, we are told, the Kingdom of God.
So we contain that which contains us.

So the departed come to light.

VII

There is a day
when the road neither
comes nor goes, and the way
is not a way but a place.

I

Whatever happens,
those who have learned
to love one another
have made their way
into the lasting world
and will not leave,
whatever happens.

II

This is the time you'd like to stay.
Not a leaf stirs. There is no sound.
The fireflies lift light from the ground.
You've shed the vanities of when
And how and why, for now. And then
The phone rings. You are called away.

III

Early in the morning, walking
in a garden in Vancouver
three thousand miles from your grave,
the sky dripping, song
sparrows singing in the borders,
I come suddenly upon
a Japanese dogwood, a tree
you loved, bowed down with bloom.
By what blessedness do I weep?

IV

The woods and pastures are joyous
in their abundance now
in a season of warmth and much rain.
We walk amid foliage, amid
song. The sheep and cattle graze
like souls in bliss (except for flies)
and lie down satisfied. Who now
can believe in winter? In winter
who could have hoped for this?

V

In a single motion the river comes and goes.
At times, living beside it, we hardly notice it
as it noses calmly along within its bounds
like the family pig. But a day comes
when it swiftens, darkens, rises, flows over
its banks, spreading its mirrors out upon
the fields of the valley floor, and then
it is like God's love or sorrow, including
at last all that had been left out.

VI

By expenditure of hope,
Intelligence, and work,
You think you have it fixed.
It is unfixed by rule.
Within the darkness, all
Is being changed, and you
Also will be changed.

Now I recall to mind
A costly year: Jane Kenyon,
Bill Lippert, Philip Sherrard,
All in the same spring dead,
So much companionship
Gone as the river goes.

And my good workhorse Nick
Dead, who called out to me
In his conclusive pain
To ask my help. I had
No help to give. And flood
Covered the cropland twice.
By summer's end there are
No more perfect leaves.

†

But won't you be ashamed
To count the passing year
At its mere cost, your debt
Inevitably paid?
For every year is costly,
As you know well. Nothing
Is given that is not
Taken, and nothing taken
That was not first a gift.

The gift is balanced by
Its total loss, and yet,
And yet the light breaks in,
Heaven seizing its moments
That are at once its own
And yours. The day ends
And is unending where
The summer tanager,
Warbler, and vireo
Sing as they move among
Illuminated leaves.

VII

For John Haines

There is a place you can go
where you are quiet,
a place of water and the light

on the water. Trees are there,
leaves, and the light
on leaves moved by air.

Birds, singing, move
among leaves, in leaf shadow.
After many years you have come

to no thought of these,
but they are themselves
your thoughts. There seems to be

little to say, less and less.
Here they are. Here you are.
Here as though gone.

None of us stays, but in the hush
where each leaf in the speech
of leaves is a sufficient syllable

the passing light finds out
surpassing freedom of its way.

VIII

Given the solemn river,
given the trees along the banks,
given the summer warmth,
the evening light—what
could have foretold the sudden
apparition of these two
speeding by as if late
for the world's end, their engine
shaking the air, breaking
the water's mirrors?
The trees and the sky hush
with dismay, and then,
upon the return of reflection,
with sorrow. How many years
of labor to become completely
displaced everywhere?

IX

What I fear most is despair
for the world and us: forever less
of beauty, silence, open air,
gratitude, unbidden happiness,
affection, unegotistical desire.

X

Tanya. Now that I am getting old,
I feel I must hurry against time to tell you
(as long ago I started out to do) everything,

though I know that there can be no end
to all there is for me to say to you even of this,
our temporary life. Sometimes it seems to me

that I am divided from you by a shadow
of incomprehension, mine or yours, or mine and yours,
or that I am caught in the misery of selfhood

forever. And I think that this must be
the lot (may God help us) of all mortals who love
each other: to know by truth that they do so,

but also by error. Often now I am reminded
that the time may come (for this is our pledge)
when you will stand by me and know

that I, though "living" still, have gone beyond
all remembering, as my father went in time
before me, or that I have gone, like my mother,

into a time of pain, drugs, and still sleep.
But I know now that in that great distance
on the edge or beyond the edge of this world

I will be growing alight with being. And (listen!)
I will be longing to come back. This
came to me in a dream, near morning,

after I had labored through the night under
this weight of earthly love. On time's edge, wakened,
shaken, light and free, I will be longing

193

to return, to seek you through the world,
to find you (recognizing you by your beauty),
to marry you, to make a place to live,

to have children and grandchildren. The light
of that place beyond time will show me the world
as perhaps Christ saw it before His birth

in the stable at Bethlehem. I will see that it is
imperfect. It will be imperfect. (To whom would love
appear but to those in most desperate need?) Yes,

we would err again. Yes, we would suffer
again. Yes, provided you would have it
so, I would do it all again.

I

Can I see the buds that are swelling
in the woods on the slopes
on the far side of the valley? I can't,
of course, nor can I see
the twinleafs and anemones
that are blooming over there
bright-scattered above the dead
leaves. But the swelling buds
and little blossoms make
a new softness in the light
that is visible all the way here.
The trees, the hills that were stark
in the old cold become now
tender, and time changes.

II

I dream of a quiet man
who explains nothing and defends
nothing, but only knows
where the rarest wildflowers
are blooming, and who goes,
and finds that he is smiling
not by his own will.

III

The spring woods hastening now
To overshadow him,
He's passing in to where
He can't see out. It charms
Mere eyesight to believe
The nearest thing not trees
Is the sky, into which
The trees reach, opening
Their luminous new leaves.
Burdened only by
A weightless shawl of shade
The lighted leaves let fall,
He seems to move within
A form unpatterned to
His eye or mind, design
Betokened to his thought
By leafshapes tossed about
Ways Indescribable
By human tongue or hand
Seem tangled here, and yet
Are brought to light, are brought
To life, and thought finds rest
Beneath a brightened tree
In which, unseen, a warbler
Feeds and sings. His song's
Small shapely melody
Comes down irregularly,
As all light's givings come.

IV

What a consolation it is, after
the explanations and the predictions
of further explanations still
to come, to return unpersuaded
to the woods, entering again
the presence of the blesséd trees.
A tree forms itself in answer
to its place and to the light.
Explain it how you will, the only
thing explainable will be
your explanation. There is
in the woods on a summer's
morning, birdsong all around
from guess where, nowhere
that rigid measure which predicts
only humankind's demise.

V

In Heaven the starry saints will wipe away
The tears forever from our eyes, but they
Must not erase the memory of our grief.
In bliss, even, there can be no relief
If we forget this place, shade-haunted, parched
Or flooded, dark or bright, where we have watched
The world always becoming what it is,
Splendor and woe surpassing happiness
Or sorrow, loss sweeping it as a floor.
This shadowed passage between door and door
Is half-lit by old words we've heard or read.
As the living recall the dead, the dead
Are joyless until they call back their lives:
Fallen like leaves, the husbands and the wives
In history's ignorant, bloody to-and-fro,
Eternally in love, and in time learning so.

VI

We travelers, walking to the sun, can't see
Ahead, but looking back the very light
That blinded us shows us the way we came,
Along which blessings now appear, risen
As if from sightlessness to sight, and we,
By blessing brightly lit, keep going toward
The blesséd light that yet to us is dark.

VII

Again I resume the long
lesson: how small a thing
can be pleasing, how little
in this hard world it takes
to satisfy the mind
and bring it to its rest.

Within the ongoing havoc
the woods this morning is
almost unnaturally still.
Through stalled air, unshadowed
light, a few leaves fall
of their own weight.

         The sky
is gray. It begins in mist
almost at the ground
and rises forever. The trees
rise in silence almost
natural, but not quite,
almost eternal, but
not quite.

       What more did I
think I wanted? Here is
what has always been.
Here is what will always
be. Even in me,
the Maker of all this
returns in rest, even
to the slightest of His works,
a yellow leaf slowly
falling, and is pleased.

VIII

The difference is a polished
blade, edgewise to the eye.
On one side gleams the sun
of time, and on the other
the never-fading light,
and so the tree that stands
full-leaved in broad day
and the darkness following
stands also in the eye
of Love and is never darkened.

The blade that divides these lights
mirrors both — is one.
Time and eternity
stand in the same day
which is now in time, and forever
now. How do we know?
We know. We know we know.
They only truly live
who are the comforted.

IX

The incarnate Word is with us,
is still speaking, is present
always, yet leaves no sign
but everything that is.

I

In the world forever one
With the informing Love
That gives its life to time,

In the day of alchemy,
Come round at last, transmuting
Corruption to pollution,

Transmuting lies to blindness,
And light to dark, the known
Destroyed in our unknowing,

Under the sun that shines
Beyond evil and good,
The goldeneye alights

On the cold river. Grace
Unasked, merely allowed,
Gleams round him on the water.

II

When we convene again
to understand the world,
the first speaker will again
point silently out the window
at the hillside in its season,
sunlit, under the snow,
and we will nod silently,
and silently stand and go.

III

As timely as a river
God's timeless life passes
Into this world. It passes
Through bodies, giving life,
And past them, giving death.
The secret fish leaps up
Into the light and is
Again darkened. The sun
Comes from the dark, it lights
The always passing river,
Shines on the great-branched tree,
And goes. Longing and dark,
We are completely filled
With breath of love, in us
Forever incomplete.

IV

The house is cold at dawn.
I wake and build the fires.
The ground is white with snow.

Snow whitens every tree.
No wind has touched the woods.
The deer stand still and look.

V

I know for a while again
the health of self-forgetfulness,
looking out at the sky through
a notch in the valley side,
the black woods wintry on
the hills, small clouds at sunset
passing across. And I know
that this is one of the thresholds
between Earth and Heaven,
from which even I may step
forth from my self and be free.

VI

(Burley Coulter, once in time)

Alone, afoot, in moonless night
Out on the world's edge with his hounds,
What was he looking to set right?
The world sings at its farthest bounds.
To know it does sets right the dark,
And so an old man found his work.

VII

Some had derided him
As unadventurous,
For he would not give up

What he had vowed to keep.
But what he vowed to keep
Even his keeping changed

And, changing, led him far
Beyond what they or he
Foresaw, and made him strange.

What he had vowed to keep
He lost, of course, and yet
Kept in his heart. The things

He vowed to keep, the things
He had in keeping changed,
The things lost in his keeping

That he kept in his heart,
These were his pilgrimage,
Were his adventure, near

And far, at home and in
The world beyond this world.

VIII·

We hear way off approaching sounds
Of rain on leaves and on the river:
O blesséd rain, bring up the grass
To the tongues of the hungry cattle.

IX

I've come down from the sky
Like some damned ghost, delayed
Too long in time enforced
By fire and by machines,
Returned at last to this
Sweet wooded slope well known
Before, where time flows on
Uncumbered as the wind.

†

No man intended this.
What came here as a gift
We use for good or ill,
For life or waste of life,
But it is as it is.
To the abandoned fields
The trees returned and grew.
They stand and grow. Time comes
To them, time goes, the trees
Stand; the only place
They go is where they are.
These wholly patient ones
Who only stand and wait
For time to come to them,
Who do not go to time,
Stand in eternity.
They stand where they belong.
They do no wrong, and they
Are beautiful. What more
Could we have thought to ask?
Here God and man have rest.

†

I've gonc too far toward time,
And now have come back home.
I stand and wait for light,
Flight-weary, growing old,
And grieved for loss of time,
For loss of time's gifts gone
With time forever, taught
By time a timeless love.

†

I stand and wait for light
To open the dark night.
I stand and wait for prayer
To come and find me here.

X

1.

We follow the dead to their graves,
and our long love follows on
beyond, crying to them, not
"Come back!" but merely "Wait!"
In waking thoughts, in dreams
we follow after, calling, "Wait!
Listen! I am older now. I know
now how it was with you
when you were old and I
was only young. I am ready
now to accompany you
in your lonely fear." And they
go on, one by one, as one
by one we go as they have gone.

2.

And yet we all are gathered
in this leftover love,
this longing become the measure
of a joy all mourners know.
An old man's mind is a graveyard
where the dead arise.

I

He wakes in darkness. All around
are sounds of shifting stones, doors
opening. As if someone had lifted
away a great weight, light
falls on him. He has been asleep or merely
gone. He has known a long suffering
of himself, himself shaped by pain,
his wound of separation he now
no longer minds, for the pain is only himself
now, grown small, become a little growing
longing joy. Joy teaches him
to rise, to stand and move out through
the opening the light has made.
He stands on the green hilltop amid
the cedars, the skewed stones, the earth all
opened doors. Half blind with light, he traces
with his forefinger the moss-grown
furrows of his name, hearing among the others
one woman's cry. She is crying and laughing,
her voice a stream of silver he seems to see:
"Oh, William, honey, is it you? Oh!"

II

Surely it will be for this: the redbud
pink, the wild plum white, yellow
trout lilies in the morning light,
the trees, the pastures turning green.
On the river, quiet at daybreak,
the reflections of the trees, as in
another world, lie across
from shore to shore. Yes, here
is where they will come, the dead,
when they rise from the grave.

III

Ask the world to reveal its quietude—
not the silence of machines when they are still,
but the true quiet by which birdsongs,
trees, bellworts, snails, clouds, storms
become what they are, and are nothing else.

IV

A mind that has confronted ruin for years
Is half or more a ruined mind. Nightmares
Inhabit it, and daily evidence
Of the clean country smeared for want of sense,
Of freedom slack and dull among the free,
Of faith subsumed in idiot luxury,
And beauty beggared in the marketplace,
And clear-eyed wisdom bleary with dispraise.

V

The wind of the fall is here.
It is everywhere. It moves
every leaf of every
tree. It is the only motion
of the river. Green leaves
grow weary of their color.
Now evening too is in the air.
The bright hawks of the day
subside. The owls waken.
Small creatures die because
larger creatures are hungry.
How superior to this
human confusion of greed
and creed, blood and fire.

VI

The question before me, now that I
am old, is not how to be dead,
which I know from enough practice,
but how to be alive, as these worn
hills still tell, and some paintings
of Paul Cézanne, and this mere
singing wren, who thinks he's alive
forever, this instant, and may be.

I

Late winter cold
over the old ground,
mud freezing under
wind and snow,
and above, on the bluffs,
the bare woods rattling
in worse wind. Weary,
an old man feeds hay
to the stock at the end
of a winter's day
in a time reduced
to work, hunger, worry,
grief, and as always
war, the killed peace
of the original world.

II

After a mild winter
the new lambs come
in a March as wet, cold,
and unforgiving as any
I remember. Night freezes
continue into April.
But the brave birds risk
a note of hope, and the bold
little wood anemones
lift their pretty blooms
into the cold above
the dead leaves. The sun
grows slowly stronger.
This Sabbath morning, I climb
again to the high woods
and sit down. Toward noon
the wind loses its edge.
Comfort comes.
I eat, and then sleep
in warmth on dry leaves
in a sheltered pocket
of the slope, the wind yet
loud beyond. I sleep
sound among young trees,
among cairns of rocks
piled up by those who cut
older trees to plant
the slope in rows. I wake
thinking of the ones who once
were here, some I knew,
others I know by stories
told and retold. I know
the hard daylong work
that once was done here:

the heat, the long enduring,
the resting and the talk
around the water jug
in shade at the row's end.
Now they are gone, and I
stay on a little while,
the trees, I hope, for longer
this time than before.
I rise from the ground now
more slowly than I once did,
thinking of those I remember
who no longer rise at all
and of those farther back
I never knew even
by story, whose names are lost,
who came by ship from places
whose names are lost.
In distance, like the trees,
the human generations
gather into a wall
nobody sees beyond.
Here where fields were
the woods are, and I come
again into the one time,
the Sabbath time, the timeless
that we pass through
and the woods grows up behind us.

III

We come at last to the dark
and enter in. We are given bodies
newly made out of their absence
from one another in the light
of the ordinary day. We come
to the space between ourselves,
the narrow doorway, and pass through
into the land of the wholly loved.

IV

The Acadian flycatcher, not
a spectacular bird, not a great
singer, is seen only when
alertly watched for. His call
is hardly a song—
a two-syllable squeak you hear
only when listened for.
His back is the color of a leaf
in shadow, his belly that
of a leaf in light. He is here
when the leaves are here, belonging
as the leaves belong, is gone when
they go. His is the voice
of this deep place among
the tiers of summer foliage
where three streams come together.
You sit and listen to the voice
of the water, and then you hear
the voice of the bird. He is saying
to his mate, to himself, to any who
may want to know: "I'm here!"

V

The cherries turn ripe, ripe,
and the birds come: red-headed
and red-bellied woodpeckers,
blue jays, cedar waxwings,
robins—beautiful, hungry, wild
in our domestic tree. I pick
with the birds, gathering the red
cherries alight among the dark
leaves, my hands so sticky
with juice the fruit will hardly
drop from them into the pail.
The birds pick as I pick, all
of us delighted in the weighty heights
—the fruit red ripe, the green leaves,
the blue sky and white clouds,
all tending to flight—making
the most of this sweetness against
the time when there will be none.
And you are to me, my love,
as a tree of ripe cherries,
and I am a wild bird high
in your branches, hungry, ready to fly!

VI

In memory: Denise Levertov

Is this the river of life
or death? Both? Both. The force
that brought us here remains
to carry us away.

Wearing its way down,
the river has left us here
on this all-slanting place:
trees, people, animals.
We stand and move a while
in air. A silent, perfect,
inaccessible world
shines sometimes at our feet.

We fall, and are carried away.
Shadowy, shadowy,
we lovers in our vale.

In its darkness the river
has worn the country
into the form it is.
The land is the water's memory.
It remembers in the light
what was made in the dark.

To know what flesh inherits,
learn the art of the little boat,
leave the solid footing,
row out upon the water.

Daylight rests brightly
on the surface of the river.
Sometimes, the air still,
world and sky rest
perfectly upon the water,
quiet as a happy dream.

Sometimes we look through it
shallowly at small fish
quick among the rocks.

In flood opaque, it is
the land's shaker, giver
and taker, maker of this place.

Sometimes when the wind
stirs, the surface is all
an impenetrable glitter, without
image or depth. Beneath
that clutter of light, our floating
eyesight, the river is dark.

Lives are lived down there
in the airless shadow where
to live long, for us, would be
to die. Excluded, we watch
the surface which divides.

From time to time we see
a long fish leap like an angel up
into common day. The dark
life shines in the air
in a cloud of bright spray.

The light flows toward the earth,
the river toward the sea,
and these do not change.
The air changes, as the mind
changes at a word from the light,
a flash from the dark.

In the curtain of wild grape
along the steep shore,
a yellow warbler appeared, disappeared,
like a bright stitch. I remember
that from forty years ago.

Bedeviled by the engines
of the utterly displaced
who come to enjoy the quiet
by making noise in it,
this is the river of the birth
of my mind and inspiration
my watching many years
here where I have made my toils.

And now I must imagine it
rising, light drawn, invisibly
up into the air.

At dusk the gray heron flies
home among the trees
and then is hidden
from everything but itself,
at peace with the day
and the coming dark.

VII

The flocking blackbirds fly across
the river, appearing above the trees
on one side, disappearing beyond
the trees on the other side. The flock
undulates in passage beneath the opening
of white sky that seems no wider
than the river. It is mid August.
The year is changing. The summer's young
are grown and strong in flight. Soon now
it will be fall. The frost will come.
To one who has watched here many years,
all of this is familiar. And yet
none of it has ever happened
before as it is happening now.

VIII

Every afternoon the old turtle
crawls up out of the river
along the trunk of a drowned tree
that slants out of the watery dark
into the sun and the wind.
In the wind and the sun he dries
and ceases to shine. He grows warm.
He looks slowly this way and that way.
He thinks slowly, and his thought
passes from satiety to hunger.
And so he lets himself sink back
down out of the air and light.

IX

All yesterday afternoon I sat
here by the river while the holiday
boats sped by. Their wake
beat on the shores, muddying
the water, their sleek hulls
rocking and pounding in the wake
of other boats, the engines filling
the air with torment. They will come
again today and again tomorrow,
for this is Labor Day weekend,
a time to celebrate with restlessness
the possibility of rest always
farther on. But this morning I came
again at first light. The river
had cleared. It lay still from bend
to bend. The night birds were passing
homeward ahead of the day. An owl
trilled once, and then a wren woke
and sang. The herons stalked
soundlessly the dusky shallows. Quietly,
quietly, the river received
the forgiveness of the new dawn.

X

Teach me work that honors Thy work,
the true economies of goods and words,
to make my arts compatible
with the songs of the local birds.

Teach me patience beyond work
and, beyond patience, the blest
Sabbath of Thy unresting love
which lights all things and gives rest.

I

The woods is white with snow.
The shy birds come and go
Between feeder and trees.
Titmice and chickadees
By right of flight survive,
I by the heavy stove.

II

The kindly faithful light returns.
Morning returns and the forgiving season.
The pastures turn green, again. Blossom
and leafbud gentle the harsh woods.
The warm breezes return to the cold river.
The phoebe returns to the porch.
And I return again to my window
where I have sat at my work all winter.
In the fortieth year of my work in this room
I sit without working and look out,
an old man, into the young light.

III LOOK OUT

Come to the window, look out, and see
the valley turning green in remembrance
of all springs past and to come, the woods
perfecting with immortal patience
the leaves that are the work of all of time,
the sycamore whose white limbs shed
the history of a man's life with their old bark,
the river under the morning's breath quivering
like the touched skin of a horse, and you will see
also the shadow cast upon it by fire, the war
that lights its way by burning the earth.

Come to your windows, people of the world,
look out at whatever you see wherever you are,
and you will see dancing upon it that shadow.
You will see that your place, wherever it is,
your house, your garden, your shop, your forest, your farm,
bears the shadow of its destruction by war
which is the economy of greed which is plunder
which is the economy of wrath which is fire.
The Lords of War sell the earth to buy fire,
they sell the water and air of life to buy fire.
They are little men grown great by willingness
to drive whatever exists into its perfect absence.
Their intention to destroy any place is solidly founded
upon their willingness to destroy every place.

Every household of the world is at their mercy,
the households of the farmer and the otter and the owl
are at their mercy. They have no mercy.
Having hate, they can have no mercy.
Their greed is the hatred of mercy.
Their pockets jingle with the small change of the poor.
Their power is their willingness to destroy

239

everything for knowledge which is money
which is power which is victory
which is ashes sown by the wind.

Leave your windows and go out, people of the world,
go into the streets, go into the fields, go into the woods
and along the streams. Go together, go alone.
Say no to the Lords of War which is Money
which is Fire. Say no by saying yes
to the air, to the earth, to the trees,
yes to the grasses, to the rivers, to the birds
and the animals and every living thing, yes
to the small houses, yes to the children. Yes.

IV

The little stream sings
in the crease of the hill.
It is the water of life. It knows
nothing of death, nothing.
And this is the morning
of Christ's resurrection.
The tomb is empty. There is
no death. Death is our illusion,
our wish to belong only
to ourselves, which is our freedom
to kill one another.
From this sleep may we too
rise, as out of the dark grave.

V

The politics of illusion, of death's money,
possesses us. This is the Hell, this
the nightmare into which Christ descended
from the cross, from which also he woke
and rose, striding godly forth, so free
that He appeared to Mary Magdalene
to be only the gardener walking about
in the new day, among the flowers.

VI

For Jonathan Williams

The yellow-throated warbler, the highest remotest voice
of this place, sings in the tops of the tallest sycamores,
but one day he came twice to the railing of my porch
where I sat at work above the river. He was too close
to see with binoculars. Only the naked eye could take him in,
a bird more beautiful than every picture of himself,
more beautiful than himself killed and preserved
by the most skilled taxidermist, more beautiful
than any human mind, so small and inexact,
could hope ever to remember. My mind became
beautiful by the sight of him. He had the beauty only
of himself alive in the only moment of his life.
He had upon him like a light the whole
beauty of the living world that never dies.

VII

This, then, is to be the way? Freedom's candle will be
snuffed out by freedom's sworn defenders, chanting
hourly the praise of freedom. Their praise
will console the free waking in their prisons
when the Bill of Rights has at last
dissolved in the indifference of the great Self
of force. When the strong have perfected their triumph
over the weak, great symphonies will still
be played in the concert halls and on the radio
to console the forgetful and the undisturbed; the doors
will still stand open at the art museums,
rewarding the oppressed for their oppression; poets
will still intone fluently their songs
of themselves, to reward the fearful for their fear. Oh,
the lofty artists of sound, of shape and color,
of words, will still accept proudly their jobs
in universities, their prizes, grants, and awards.
On the day that ugliness is perfected in rubble
and blood, beauty and the love of beauty will
still be praised by those well paid to praise it.

†

When they cannot speak freely in defiance
of wealth self-elected to righteousness,
let the arts of pleasure and beauty cease.
Let every poet and singer of joy be dumb.
When those in power by owning all the words
have made them mean nothing, let silence
speak for us. When freedom's light goes out, let color
drain from all paintings into gray puddles
on the museum floor. When every ear awaits only
the knock on the door in the dark midnight,
let all the orchestras sound just one long note of woe.

VIII

All that patriotism requires, and all that it can be,
is eagerness to maintain intact and incorrupt
the founding principles of the nation, and to preserve
undiminished the land and the people. If national conduct
forsakes these aims, it is one's patriotic duty
to say so and to oppose. What else have we to live for?

IX

After the campaign of the killing machines
the place, which could be any place,
was heaped with corpses, dismembered and stinking.
For them the great simplification had come
and the fear of suffering, at least, at last was finished.
But the one we have remembered longest was the one
who survived, who was pulled free,
bloody with his own blood and the blood
of the reeking dead who, dying, had sheltered him
—the one who to his horror found that the little light
of our world is beautiful and holy,
and he must live.

X

But do the Lords of War in fact
hate the world? That would be easy
to bear, if so. If they hated
their children and the flowers
that grow in the warming light,
that would be easy to bear. For then
we could hate the haters
and be right. What is hard
is to imagine the Lords of War
may love the things that they destroy.

XI

It is late November, Thanksgiving,
and the slow rain falls as all day
it has fallen. The mists drift
in the treetops along Camp Branch.
The ewe flock grazes the green slope
as in a dream of a painting
by Samuel Palmer. There is no wind.
It is completely quiet. From the distance
comes only the sound of the branch
flowing in its wooded hollow, old,
old, and new, unidentifying the day
and the man giving his thanks.

2004

I

(After the painting Jacob's Dream *by William Blake
and Genesis 28: 11–17)*

A young man leaving home
For long years to be gone
Might fall asleep and dream,
His head upon a stone.

A stair appears that bends
In spiral toward the light,
The bright Orb where it ends,
Though he sleeps through the night,

Darkened, below the stars.
Angels in constant motion
Walk up and down the stairs.
Delight and clear devotion

Make graceful all they do.
The light and dark are bound,
Heaven to all below,
Bright stair and stony ground

In one light joined. In sleep
The dreamer wakes. He sees
Above the stars the deep
Of Heaven opened. Is

He living, then, his part
Of Heaven's earthly life?
And what shall be the art
By which this sight can live?

Darkened upon the earth,
He fills with light, is made
A witness to high Truth
And so a man afraid.

His land—this meager sod,
These stones, this low estate—
Is the household of God.
And it is Heaven's gate.

II

They come singly, the little streams,
Out of their solitude. They bear
In their rough fall a spate of gleams
That glance and dance in morning air.

They come singly, and coming go
Ever downward toward the river
Into whose dark abiding flow
They come, now quieted, together.

In dark they mingle and are made
At one with light in highest flood
Embodied and inhabited,
The budded branch as red as blood.

III

They are fighting again the war to end war,
and the ewe flock, bred in October, brings forth
in March. This so far remains, this pain
and renewal, whatever war is being fought.
We go through the annual passage of birth
and death, triumph and heartbreak, love
and exasperation, mud, milk, mucus, and blood.
Yet once more the young ewe stands with her lambs
in the dawnlight, the lambs well-suckled
and dry. There is no happiness like this.

The window again welcomes in the light
of lengthening days. The river in its old groove
passes again beneath opening leaves.
In their brevity, between cold and shade,
flowers again brighten the woods floor.

This then may be the prayer without ceasing,
this beauty and gratitude, this moment.

IV

(Jayber Crow in old age)

To think of gathering all
the sorrows of Port William
into myself, and so
sparing the others:
What freedom! What joy!

V

I built a timely room beside the river,
The slope beneath descending to the water.
Some mornings it is vibrant with the glance
Of sunlight brightened on the little waves
The wind drives shoreward, stirring leaves and branches
Over the roof also. It is a room
Of pictures and of memories of some
Who are no more in time, and of the absent
And of the present the unresting thoughts.
It is a room as timely as the body,
As frail, to shelter love's eternal work,
Always unfinished, here at water's edge,
The work of beauty, faith, and gratitude
Eternally alive in time. Around
The walls the trees like waves, like men,
Come up, come up, expend themselves, and die.
The water shines back the unending sky.

VI

Up in the blown-down woods
you try to imagine the tornado
cracking through the trees
while you slept, branches
and birds' eggs whirling
in the dark. You can't do it.
You can imagine the place
as it was, and as it is.
The moment of transformation,
the presence of creation,
itself is beyond your reach.

VII

Dee Rice Amyx, 1910–2004

A gracious lady came to us
and favored us by receiving
kindly our care of her
at the end of all her days.

She was a lady made graceful
beyond what we had known
by the welcome she gave to death,
her guest, whom she made unfearful

by her fearlessness, having no further
use for herself as we had known her.

VIII

It takes all time to show eternity,
The longest shine of every perishing spark,
And every word and cry of every tongue
Must form the Word that calls the darkest dark

Of this world to its lasting dawn. Toward
That rising hour we bear our single hearts
Estranged as islands parted in the sea,
Our broken knowledge and our scattered arts.

As separate as fireflies or night windows,
We piece a foredream of the gathered light
Infinitely small and great to shelter all,
Silenced into song, blinded into sight.

IX

I mistook your white head for a flower
down there among the tall grasses
and flowers of the garden border.
And then I knew you, your years
upon you like a crown of glory.

X

An old man, who has been on many days
a man of the woods, has come again
to this place where three streams join, where
once he sat in his pleasure under the tall trees
and the world's light shone from every leaf,

where now a great wind has blown, and he
alone is still upright, his old companions
all broken and brought down. It is the place
of endings he has come to, of the world's end
that is always near, always here. "Farewell,"

he says. "Welcome," he says. For it is the place
also of the world's beginning, ever here, for here
there is again a living darkness underfoot,
a small wind is moving farther into time, and here
he is, astir among the fallen.

I

I know that I have life
only insofar as I have love.

I have no love
except it come from Thee.

Help me, please, to carry
this candle against the wind.

II

They gather like an ancestry
in the centuries behind us:
the killed by violence, the dead
in war, the "acceptable losses"—
killed by custom in self-defense,
by way of correction, in revenge,
for love of God, for the glory
of the world, for peace; killed
for pride, lust, envy, anger,
covetousness, gluttony, sloth,
and fun. The strewn carcasses
cease to feed even the flies,
the stench passes from them,
the earth folds in the bones
like salt in a batter.

And we have learned
nothing. "Love your enemies,
bless them that curse you,
do good to them that hate you"—
it goes on regardless, reasonably:
the always uncompleted
symmetry of just reprisal,
the angry word, the boast
of superior righteousness,
hate in Christ's name,
scorn for the dead, lies
for the honor of the nation,
centuries bloodied and dismembered
for ideas, for ideals,
for the love of God!

III

"Are you back to normal?" asks
my old friend, ill himself, after I,
who have been ill, am well. "Yes,
the gradient of normality now
being downward." For when I walk
now from rock to rock in the tumble
of Camp Branch, under the trees,
the singing stream, the stream
of light that all my life
has drawn me as it has drawn
the ever-renewing waters, I clamber
where I used to leap, where once I could
have been a ghost for all the care
I paid to flesh and bone until
some hunger turned me home.

IV

We were standing by the road,
seven of us and a small boy.
We had just rescued a yellow swallowtail
disabled on the pavement when a car
approached too fast. I turned to make sure
of the boy, and my old border collie
Nell, too slow coming across,
was hit, broken all to pieces, and died
at once, while the car sped on.
And I cried, not thinking what
I meant, "God damn!" And I did wish
all automobiles in Hell,
where perhaps they already are.

V

Nell's small grave, opening
at the garden's edge to receive her
out of this world's sight forever,
reopens many graves. Digging,
the old man grieves for his old dog
with all the grief he knows,
which seems again to be approaching
enough, though he knows there is more.

VI

How simple to be dead! — the only
simplification there is, in fact, Thoreau
to the contrary notwithstanding.
Nell lay in her grave utterly still
under the falling earth, the world
all astir above, a million leaves
alive in the wind, and what do we know?

VII

I know I am getting old and I say so,
but I don't think of myself as an old man.
I think of myself as a young man
with unforeseen debilities. Time is neither
young nor old, but simply new, always
counting, the only apocalypse. And the clouds
—no mere measure or geometry, no cubism,
can account for clouds or, satisfactorily, for bodies.
There is no science for this, or art either.
Even the old body is new—who has known it
before?—and no sooner new than gone, to be
replaced by a body yet older and again new.
The clouds are rarely absent from our sky
over this humid valley, and there is a sycamore
that I watch as, growing on the riverbank,
it forecloses the horizon, like the years
of an old man. And you, who are as old
almost as I am, I love as I loved you
young, except that, old, I am astonished
at such a possibility, and am duly grateful.

VIII

I tremble with gratitude
for my children and their children
who take pleasure in one another.

At our dinners together, the dead
enter and pass among us
in living love and in memory.

And so the young are taught.

IX

Here in the woods near
the road where the public lives
the birds are at their daily work,
singing, feeding, feeding
the young, as if the road
does not exist.
          Here
by the loud road, populous
and vacant, there is quiet
where birds are singing.
                The birds
are waiting to sing in the trees
that will grow in the quiet
that will come when the last
of the dire machines has passed,
burning the world, and the burning
has ceased.
         And so am I.

X

Mowing the hillside pasture—where
the flowers of Queen Anne's lace

float above the grass, the milkweeds
flare and bee balm, cut, spices

the air, the butterflies light and fly
from bloom to bloom, the hot

sun dazes the sky, the woodthrushes
sound their flutes from the deep shade

of the woods nearby—these iron teeth
chattering along the slope astound

the vole in her low run and bring down
the field sparrow's nest cunningly hung

between two stems, the young long flown.
The mower moves between the beauty

of the half-wild growth and the beauty
of growth reduced, smooth as a lawn,

revealing again the slope shaped of old
by the wearing of water and, later, the wear

of human will, hoof and share and wheel
hastening the rain's work, so that the shape

revealed is the shape of wounds healed,
covered with grass and clover and the blessèd

flowers. The mower's work too is beautiful,
granting rest and health to his mind.

He drives the long traverses of the healed
and healing slant. He sweats and gives thanks.

XI

My young grandson rides with me
as I mow the day's first swath
in the hillside pasture,
and then he rambles the woods beyond
the field's edge, emerging
from the trees to wave, and I wave back,

remembering that I too once
played at a field's edge and waved
to an old workman who went mowing by,
waving back to me as he passed.

XII

If we have become a people incapable
of thought, then the brute-thought
of mere power and mere greed
will think for us.

If we have become incapable
of denying ourselves anything,
then all that we have
will be taken from us.

If we have no compassion,
we will suffer alone, we will suffer
alone the destruction of ourselves.

These are merely the laws of this world
as known to Shakespeare, as known to Milton:

When we cease from human thought,
a low and effective cunning
stirs in the most inhuman minds.

XIII

Eternity is not infinity.
It is not a long time.
It does not begin at the end of time.
It does not run parallel to time.
In its entirety it always was.
In its entirety it will always be.
It is entirely present always.

XIV

God, how I hate the names
of the body's chemicals and anatomy,
the frore and glum department
of its parts, each alone in the scattering
of the experts of Babel.
                    The body
is a single creature, whole,
its life is one, never less than one, or more,
so is its world, and so
are two bodies in their love for one another
one. In ignorance of this
we talk ourselves to death.

XV

The painter Harlan Hubbard said
that he was painting Heaven when
the places he painted merely were
the Campbell or the Trimble County
banks of the Ohio, or farms
and hills where he had worked or roamed:
a house's gable and roofline
rising from a fold in the hills,
trees bearing snow, two shanty boats
at dawn, immortal light upon
the flowing river in its bends.
And these were Heavenly because
he never saw them clear enough
to satisfy his love, his need
to see them all again, again.

XVI

I am hardly an ornithologist,
nevertheless I live among the birds
and on the best days my mind
is with them, partaking of their nature
which is earthly and airy.

I live with the heavenly swallows
who fly for joy (to live, yes, but also for joy)
as they pass again and again over
the river, feeding, drinking, bathing
joyfully as they fly.

Sometimes my thoughts are up there
with the yellow-throated warbler, high
among the white branches and gray-green
foliage of the sycamores, singing
as he feeds among the lights and shadows.

A ringing in my ears from hearing
too many of the wrong things
surrounds my head some days
like a helmet, and yet I hear the birds
singing: the song sparrow by the water,
the mockingbird, whose song so beautiful
flings him into the air.

Song comes from a source unseen
as if from a stirring leaf, but I know
the note before I see the bird.
It is a Carolina wren whose good cheer
never falters all year long.

Into the heat, into the smells
of horse sweat, man sweat, wilting
foliage, stirred earth,
the song of the wood thrush flows
cool from the dark woods.

I hear the sounds of wings.
What man can abide the rule
of "the market" when he hears,
in his waking, in his sleep,
the sound of wings?

In the night I hear the owls
trilling near and far;
it is my dream that calls,
my dream that answers.

Sometimes as I sit quiet
on my porch above the river
a warbler will present himself,
parula or yellow-throated or prothonotary,
perfect beauty in finest detail,
seeming as unaware
of me as I am aware of him.

Or, one never knows quite when,
the waxwings suddenly appear,
numerous and quiet, not here
it seems until one looks,
as though called forth, like angels,
by willingness for them to be.

Or it has come to be September
and the blackbirds are flocking.
They pass through the riverbank trees
in one direction erratically
like leaves in the wind.

Or it is June. The martins are nesting.
The he-bird has the fiercest
countenance I have ever seen. He drops
out of the sky as a stone falls
and then he breaks his fall and alights
light on the housetop
as though gravity were not.

Think of it! To fly
by mere gift, without the clamor
and stain of our inert metal,
in perfect trust.

It is the Sabbath of the birds
that so moves me. They belong
in their ever-returning song, in their flight,
in their faith in the upholding air,
to the Original World. They are above us
and yet of us, for those who fly
fall, like those who walk.

XVII

Hardly escaping the limitless machines
that balk his thoughts and torment his dreams,
the old man goes to his own
small place of peace, a patch of trees
he has lived from many years,
its gifts of a few fence posts and boards,
firewood for winter, some stillness
in which to know and wait. Used
and yet whole this dear place is, whole
by its own nature and by his need.
While he lives it will be whole,
and after him, God willing, another
will follow in that membership
that craves the wholeness of the world
despite all human loss and blame.

In the lengthening shadow he has climbed
again to the ridgetop and across
to the westward slope to see the ripe
light of autumn in the turning trees,
the twilight he must go by now
that only grace can give. Thus far
he keeps the old sectarian piety:
By grace we live. But he can go
no further. Having known the grace
that for so long has kept this world,
haggard as it is, as we have made it,
we cannot rest, we must be stirring
to keep this gift dwelling among us,
eternally alive in time. This
is the great work, no other, none harder,
none nearer rest or more beautiful.

XVIII

A hawk in flight
The clearing sky
A young man's thought
An old man's cry

XIX

Born by our birth
Here on the earth
Our flesh to wear
Our death to bear

I

If there are a "chosen few"
then I am not one of them,
if an "elect," well then
I have not been elected.
I am one who is knocking
at the door. I am one whose foot
is on the bottom rung.
But I know that Heaven's
bottom rung is Heaven
though the ladder is standing
on the earth where I work
by day and at night sleep
with my head upon a stone.

II   OLD MAN JAYBER CROW

Many I loved as man and boy
Are gone beyond all that I know,
Fallen leaves under falling rain,
Except Christ raise them up again.
I know my blessings by their cost,
Thus is the pride of man made low.
To ease the sorrow of my thoughts,
Though I'm too weary now and slow,
I'd need to dance all night for joy.

III   THE BOOK OF CAMP BRANCH

Camp Branch, my native stream,
forever unreturning flows
from the town down to Cane Run
which flows to the river. It is
my native descent, my native
walk, my native thought
that stays and goes, passing
ever downward toward the sea.

Its sound is a song that flings up
light to the undersides of leaves.
Its song and light are a way
of walking, a way of thought
moved by sound and sight.

It flows as deep in its hollow
as it can go, far down as it has
worn its way. Passing down
over its plunder of rocks, it makes
an irregular music. Here
is what I want to know. Here
is what I am trying to say.

O brave Ross Feld, here is
no "fortification against time."
Here the fort has fallen
and the water passes its benediction
over the shards, singing!

⚘

How much delight I've known
in navigating down the flow
by stepping stones, by sounding

stones, by words too that are
stepping and sounding stones.

Going down stone by stone,
the song of the water changes,
changing the way I walk
which changes my thought
as I go. Stone to stone
the stream flows. Stone to stone
the walker goes. The words
stand stone still until
the flow moves them, changing
the sound—a new word—
a new place to step or stand.

❧

In the notch of Camp Branch
the footing changes, year
to year, sometimes
day to day, as the surges
of the stream move the rocks.
Every walk, as Archie Ammons
said, "is a new walk." And so

go slow. Let the mind
step with the feet
as the stream steps
downward over the rocks,
nowhere anywhere
but where it is.

❧

In the crease of its making
the steep stream gathers
the seeps that come silently

down from the wooded slants.
Only there at the rockbed
of the branch do the waters break
into light, into singing

of water flowing over rocks
which, in its motion, the water
moves. And so, singing, the song
changes, moved by music
harsh and crude: splashes,
slubbers, chuckles, and warbles,
the hollow tones of a bell,
a sustained pour, the small
fall steady as a column.

Sometimes, quieted—if you
stand while it flows—it seems
to meditate upon itself
and the hill's long changing
under sun and rain.

☙

A changing song,
a changing walk,
a changing thought.

A sounding stone,
a stepping stone,
a word
that is a sounding and a stepping
stone.

A language that is a stream flowing
and is a man's thoughts as he
walks and thinks beside the stream.

His thoughts will hold
if the words will hold, if each
is a weight-bearing stone
placed by the flow
in the flow. The language too

descends through time, subserving
false economy, heedless power,
blown with the gas of salesmanship,
rattled with the sale of needless war,

worn by the mere unhearing
babble of thoughtlessness,
and must return to its own
downward flow by the flowing
water, the muttered syllables,
the measureless music, the stream
flowing and singing, the man
walking and thinking, balanced
on unsure footholds
in the flowing stream.

❦

"Make sense," I told myself,
the song of the tumbling waters
in my ears. The sense you make
may make its way along the stream,
but it will not be the stream's sense
you make, nor yet your own
quite, for the flux of language
will make its claim too
upon the sense you make.

The words fall at last
onto the page, the turning leaf
in the Book of Camp Branch

in time's stream. As the eye,
as the mind, move from
moving water to turning page,
what is lost? What, worse,
is lost if the words falsify
the stream in your walk beside it?
To be carried or to resist
you must be a stone
in the way. You must be
a stone rolled away.

⟡

The song changes by singing
into a different song.
It sings by falling. The water
descending in its old groove
wears it new. The words descending
to the page render the possible
into the actual, by wear,
for better or worse, renew
the wearied mind. This is only
the lowly stream of Camp Branch,
but every stream is lowly.
Only low in the land does
the water flow. It goes
to seek the level that is lowest,
the silence that gathers
many songs, the darkness
made of many lights,
and then by the sun is raised
again into the air.

IV

The times are disgusting enough,
surely, for those who long for peace
and truth. But self-disgust
also is an injury: the coming
of bodily uncertainty with age
and wear, forgetfulness of things
that ought to be remembered,
remembrance of things best forgot.
Forgive this fragmentary life.

V

Little stream, Camp Branch, flowing
through the ever-renewing
woods on the steep slopes,
by what name did the Shawnee
call you? We live briefly in time
longer than we will live to know.
When we who know you by name
are gone, what will they call you?
When our nation has fallen as all
things fall, when the Constitution
is only another paper god, prayed to
and lied to by only another
autocrat, what will they call you?
When our kind has gone
as all things go, and you remain,
your tumbles catching and returning
light to the air as beautifully
as before, will only the angels
name you and praise you then?

VI

O saints, if I am eligible for this prayer,
though less than worthy of this dear desire,
and if your prayers have influence in Heaven,
let my place there be lower than your own.
I know how you longed, here where you lived
as exiles, for the presence of the essential
Being and Maker and Knower of all things.
But because of my unruliness, or some erring
virtue in me never rightly schooled,
some error clear and dear, my life
has not taught me your desire for flight:
dismattered, pure, and free. I long
instead for the Heaven of creatures, of seasons,
of day and night. Heaven enough for me
would be this world as I know it, but redeemed
of our abuse of it and one another. It would be
the Heaven of knowing again. There is no marrying
in Heaven, and I submit; even so, I would like
to know my wife again, both of us young again,
and I remembering always how I loved her
when she was old. I would like to know
my children again, all my family, all my dear ones,
to see, to hear, to hold, more carefully
than before, to study them lingeringly as one
studies old verses, committing them to heart
forever. I would like again to know my friends,
my old companions, men and women, horses
and dogs, in all the ages of our lives, here
in this place that I have watched over all my life
in all its moods and seasons, never enough.
I will be leaving how many beauties overlooked?
A painful Heaven this would be, for I would know
by it how far I have fallen short. I have not

paid enough attention, have not been grateful
enough. And yet this pain would be the measure
of my love. In eternity's once and now, pain would
place me surely in the Heaven of my earthly love.

VII

Before we kill another child
for righteousness' sake, to serve
some blissful killer's sacred cause,
some bloody patriot's anthem
and his flag, let us leave forever
our ancestral lands, our holy books,
our god thoughtified to the mean
of our smallest selves. Let us go
to the graveyard and lie down
forever among the speechless stones.

VIII

*We might as well require a man to wear still the coat which
fitted him when a boy as civilized society to remain ever under
the regimen of their barbarous ancestors.*
Thomas Jefferson to Samuel Kercheval, July 12, 1816

How can we be so superior
to "our barbarous ancestors"?
The truth will never be complete
in any mind or time. It will never
be reduced to an explanation.
What you have is only a sack of fragments
never to be filled: old bones, fossils,
facts, scraps of writing, sprawls of junk.
You know yourself only poorly and in part,
the best and the worst maybe forgotten.
However you arrange the pieces, however
authentic, a story is what you'll have,
an artifact, for better or worse.
So go ahead. Gather your findings into
a plausible arrangement. Make a story.
Show how love and joy, beauty and goodness
shine out amongst the rubble.

IX

"That's been an oak tree a long time,"
said Arthur Rowanberry. How long a time
we did not know. The oak meant,
as Art meant, that we were lost
in time, in which the oak and we had come
and would go. Nobody knows what
to make of this. It was as if,
there in the Sabbath morning light,
we both were buried or unborn while
the oak lived, or it would fall
while we stood. But Art, who had
the benefit of not too much education,
not too many days pressed between pages
or framed in a schoolhouse window,
is long fallen now, though he stands
in my memory still as he stood
in time, or stands in Heaven,
and a few of his memories remain
a while as memories of mine. To be
on horseback with him and free,
lost in time, found in place, early
Sunday morning, was plain delight.
We had ridden over all his farm,
along field edges, through the woods,
in search of ripe wild fruit, and found
none, for all our pains, and yet
"We didn't find what we were looking for,"
said Arthur Rowanberry, pleased,
"but haven't we seen some fine country!"

"When you get the time to do it and you drive up here and leave your truck and walk into the woods and stay a while in a pretty place where you don't hear no noise and nothing's bothering you, and you go back the next week and that place is not even there, that's hard."

Joe Begley (1919–2000) of Blackey, Kentucky,
speaking of mountain-removal coal mining

I

I dream by night the horror
That I oppose by day.
The nation in its error
And by its work and play

Destroys its land, pollutes
Its streams, and desecrates
Air and light. From the roots
It dies upward, our rights,

Divinely given, plundered
And sold by purchased power
That dies from the head downward,
Marketed hour by hour.

The market is a grave
Where goods lie dead that ought
To live and grow and thrive,
The dear world sold and bought

To be destroyed by fire,
Forest and soil and stone.
The conscience put to hire
Rules over flesh and bone.

To take the coal to burn
They overturn the world
And all the world has worn
Of grace, of health. The gnarled,

Clenched, and forever shut
Fist of their greed makes small
The great Life. Hollowed out,
The soul like the green hill

Yields to the force of dearth.
The crack in the despot's skull
Descends into the earth,
And what was bright turns dull.

II

The nation is a boat,
as some have said, ourselves
its passengers. How troubling
now to ride it drifting
down the flow from the old
high vision of dignity, freedom,
holy writ of habeas corpus,
and the land's abundance—down
to waste, want, fear, tyranny,
torture, caricature
of vision in a characterless time,
while the abyss whirls below.

⸙

To save yourself heartwhole
in life, in death, go back
upstream, if you have to swim
ashore and walk. Walk
upstream along the bank
of the Kentucky River, the bank
of Cane Run, and step from
stone to stone up Camp Branch
through the cut down, longtime
returning woods. Go back
through the narrowing valleys
to the waters of origin, the dry
leaves, the bare wintering trees,
the dead, the unreturning.
Go from the corrupted nation
to the ruining country. With the land
again make common cause.
In loving it, be free.
Diminished as it is,

grant it your grief and care,
whole in heart, in mind
free, though you die or live.
So late, begin again.

✦

The abyss of no-meaning—what
can prevail against it? Love
for the water in its standing
fall through the hill's wrist
from the town down to the river.
There is no love but this,
and it extends from Heaven
to the land destroyed,
to the hurt man in his cage,
to the dead man in his grave.

✦

Shall we do without hope? Some days
there will be none. But now
to the dead and dry woods floor
they come again, the first
flowers of the year, the assembly
of the faithful, the beautiful,
wholly given to being.
And in this long season
of machines and mechanical will
there have been small human acts
of compassion, acts of care, work
flowerlike in selfless loveliness.
Leaving hope to the dark
and to a better day,
receive these beauties freely
given, and give thanks.

III

Yes, though hope is our duty,
let us live a while without it
to show ourselves we can.
Let us see that, without hope,
we still are well. Let hopelessness
shrink us to our proper size.
Without it we are half as large
as yesterday, and the world
is twice as large. My small
place grows immense as I walk
upon it without hope.
Our springtime rue anemones
as I walk among them, hoping
not even to live, are beautiful
as Eden, and I their kinsman
am immortal in their moment.

Out of charity let us pray
for the great ones of politics
and war, the intellectuals,
scientists, and advisors,
the golden industrialists,
the CEOs, that they too
may wake to a day without hope
that in their smallness they
may know the greatness of Earth
and Heaven by which they so far
live, that they may see
themselves in their enemies,
and from their great wants fallen
know the small immortal
joys of beasts and birds.

IV

In our consciousness of time
we are doomed to the past.
The future we may dream of
but can know it only after
it has come and gone.
The present too we know
only as the past. When
we say, "This now is
present, the heat, the breeze,
the rippling water," it is past.
Before we knew it, before
we said "now," it was gone.

If the only time we live
is the present, and if the present
is immeasurably short (or
long), then by the measure
of the measurers we don't
exist at all, which seems
improbable, or we are
immortals, living always
in eternity, as from time to time
we hear, but rarely know.

You see the rainbow and the new-leafed
woods bright beneath, you see
the otters playing in the river
or the swallows flying, you see
a belovèd face, mortal
and alive, causing the heart
to sway in the rift between beats
where we live without counting,
where we have forgotten time
and have forgotten ourselves,

where eternity has seized us
as its own. This breaks
open the little circles
of the humanly known and believed,
of the world no longer existing,
letting us live where we are,
as in the deepest sleep also
we are entirely present,
entirely trusting, eternal.

Is it concentration of the mind,
our unresting counting
that leaves us standing
blind in our dust?
In time we are present only
by forgetting time.

V

Those who use the world assuming
their knowledge is sufficient
destroy the world. The forest
is mangled for the sale
of a few sticks, or is bulldozed
into a stream and covered over
with the earth it once stood
upon. The stream turns foul,
killing the creatures that once
lived from it. Industrial humanity,
an alien species, lives by death.
In the clutter of facts, the destroyers
leave behind them one big story,
of the world and the world's end,
that they don't know. They know
names and little stories. But the names
of everything are not everything.
The story of everything, told,
is only a little story. They don't know
the languages of the birds
who pass northward, feeding
through the treetops early
in May, kept alive by knowledge
never to be said in words.
Hang down your head. This
is our hope: Words emerge
from silence, the silence remains.

VI

It is hard to have hope. It is harder as you grow old,
for hope must not depend on feeling good
and there is the dream of loneliness at absolute midnight.
You also have withdrawn belief in the present reality
of the future, which surely will surprise us,
and hope is harder when it cannot come by prediction
any more than by wishing. But stop dithering.
The young ask the old to hope. What will you tell them?
Tell them at least what you say to yourself.

Because we have not made our lives to fit
our places, the forests are ruined, the fields eroded,
the streams polluted, the mountains overturned. Hope
then to belong to your place by your own knowledge
of what it is that no other place is, and by
your caring for it as you care for no other place, this
place that you belong to though it is not yours,
for it was from the beginning and will be to the end.

Belong to your place by knowledge of the others who are
your neighbors in it: the old man, sick and poor,
who comes like a heron to fish in the creek,
and the fish in the creek, and the heron who manlike
fishes for the fish in the creek, and the birds who sing
in the trees in the silence of the fisherman
and the heron, and the trees that keep the land
they stand upon as we too must keep it, or die.

This knowledge cannot be taken from you by power
or by wealth. It will stop your ears to the powerful
when they ask for your faith, and to the wealthy
when they ask for your land and your work.
Answer with knowledge of the others who are here

and of how to be here with them. By this knowledge
make the sense you need to make. By it stand
in the dignity of good sense, whatever may follow.

Speak to your fellow humans as your place
has taught you to speak, as it has spoken to you.
Speak its dialect as your old compatriots spoke it
before they had heard a radio. Speak
publicly what cannot be taught or learned in public.

Listen privately, silently to the voices that rise up
from the pages of books and from your own heart.
Be still and listen to the voices that belong
to the streambanks and the trees and the open fields.
There are songs and sayings that belong to this place,
by which it speaks for itself and no other.

Found your hope, then, on the ground under your feet.
Your hope of Heaven, let it rest on the ground
underfoot. Be lighted by the light that falls
freely upon it after the darkness of the nights
and the darkness of our ignorance and madness.
Let it be lighted also by the light that is within you,
which is the light of imagination. By it you see
the likeness of people in other places to yourself
in your place. It lights invariably the need for care
toward other people, other creatures, in other places
as you would ask them for care toward your place and you.

No place at last is better than the world. The world
is no better than its places. Its places at last
are no better than their people while their people
continue in them. When the people make
dark the light within them, the world darkens.

VII

In time a man disappears
from his lifelong fields, from
the streams he has walked beside,
from the woods where he sat and waited.
Thinking of this, he seems to
miss himself in those places
as if always he has been there,
watching for himself to return.
But first he must disappear,
and this he foresees with hope,
with thanks. Let others come.

VIII

Poem, do not raise your voice.
Be a whisper that says "There!"
where the stream speaks to itself
of the deep rock of the hill
it has carved its way down to
in flowing over them, "There!"
where the sun enters and the tanager
flares suddenly on the lighted branch,
"There!" where the aerial columbine
brightens on its slender stalk.
Walk, poem. Watch, and make no noise.

IX

I go by a field where once
I cultivated a few poor crops.
It is now covered with young trees,
for the forest that belongs here
has come back and reclaimed its own.
And I think of all the effort
I have wasted and all the time,
and of how much joy I took
in that failed work and how much
it taught me. For in so failing
I learned something of my place,
something of myself, and now
I welcome back the trees.

X

I love the passing light
upon this valley now green
in early summer as I watch
late in life. And upon the one
by whom I live, who is herself
a light, the light is passing
as she works in the garden
in the quiet. The past light
I love, but even more
the passing light. To this
love, we give our work.

XI

The sounds of engines leave the air.
The Sunday morning silence comes
at last. At last I know the presence
of the world made without hands,
the creatures that have come to be
out of their absence. Calls
of flicker and jay fill the clear
air. Titmice and chickadees feed
among the green and the dying leaves.
Gratitude for the gifts of all the living
and the unliving, gratitude which is
the greatest gift, quietest of all,
passes to me through the trees.

XII

Learn by little the desire for all things
which perhaps is not desire at all
but undying love which perhaps
is not love at all but gratitude
for the being of all things which
perhaps is not gratitude at all
but the maker's joy in what is made,
the joy in which we come to rest.

XIII

"The past above, the future below
and the present pouring down . . ."
wrote Dr. Williams. Is that
correct? Or is the future above
and the past below?
                    The stream
that is departing from itself as
it was is above and is the past.
The stream that is coming to itself
as it will be is below and is
the future. Or:
                    The stream yet
to come is above and is the future.
The stream that has gone by
is below and is the past.

In its riddles in the world
in the mind in the world
the stream is the stream
beyond words, beginning nowhere,
ending nowhere.
                    It falls as rain.
It flows in all its length. It enters
finally the sea. It rises into the air.
It falls as rain. To the watcher
on the shore, it comes and it
goes.
        The immeasurable, untestable,
irrecoverable moment of its passing
is the present, always already
past before we can say that it is
present, that it was the future
flowing into the past or is
the past flowing into the future

or both at once into the present
that is ever-passing and eternal,
the instantaneous, abounding life.

I

After the bitter nights
and the gray, cold days
comes a bright afternoon.
I go into the creek valley
and there are the horses, the black
and the white, lying in the warm
shine on a bed of dry hay.
They lie side by side,
identically posed as a painter
might imagine them:
heads up, ears and eyes
alert. They are beautiful in the light
and in the warmth happy. Such
harmonies are rare. This is
not the way the world
is. It is a possibility
nonetheless deeply seeded
within the world. It is
the way the world is sometimes.

II

A man's desire, overwhelming
as it may seem, is no greater
than that of the male chickadee
or the yellow-throated warbler
at his high ecstatic song, no smaller
than that of the bull elephant
or whale. And so we come,
whichever way we turn, to plentitude.
The fullness of a cup equals
that of the sea—unless the mind
conceive of more, longing for women
in disregard of the limit
of singularity, gluttonous beyond
hunger, greedy for money in excess
of goods, lusting for Heaven
in excess, not only of our worth
which would be most humbling,
but of any known human power
of delectation. And so the mind
grows a big belly, a sack full
of the thought of more, and the whole
structure of enough, of life itself,
which is never more or less
than enough, falls in pieces.
In the name of more we destroy
for coal the mountain and its forest
and so choose the insatiable flame
over the green leaf that within our care
would return to us unendingly
until the end of time.

III

Inside its bends, the river
builds the land, outside
it frets the land away.
This is unjust only
in a limited view. Forever
it doesn't matter, is only
the world's way, the give
and take, the take and
give we suffer in order
to live. This household
of my work, ungainly on
its stilts, stands outside
the bend, and the river wears
near and near, flow
outlasting the standing firm.
Trees once here are gone,
the slope they stood upon
gone. I needed what is lost,
although I love as well
the flow that took it. Now
spring is coming, the redbird's
peal rings from the thicket,
the pair exchanges like
a kiss a seed from the feeder,
and this is timeless. But a day
in time will come when this
house will give way, the walls
lean and fall. Shattered will be
my window's rectitude.

IV

A man is walking in a field
and everywhere at his feet
in the short grass of April
the small purple violets
are in bloom. As the man walks
the ground drops away,
the sunlight of day becomes
a sort of darkness in which
the lights of the flowers rise
up around him like
fireflies or stars in a sort
of sky through which he walks.

V

How many of your birthdays
I have by now been
glad of! And all that time
I've been trying to tell you
how with you was born
my truest life and most
desired, the better man
by your birth I am, however
fallen short. I'll never
get it right by half.
Between us, by now, what
is more telling than the silence
in which once more an old
redbud simply blooms?

VI   THE LOCUSTS

For the third time since the first
summer we were married, they've come
again. Having stayed seventeen years
in the dark ground, they rise as if
only a night has passed, uttering
by instruction deep and great
as their long delay their ancient call:
"Pha-a-a-a-a-a-a-a-*raoh*!" as
Art Rowanberry said they say,
remembering their days as a plague
in Egypt. And yet they come young
to the light from time older than Pharaoh.
They must come young or not at all.
Our sleeps, like theirs, have carried us
through many darknesses, to wake
to plagues of our time, minds willfully
mechanical, great power ignorant
and greedy, our own complicity,
but waking to the same light the locusts
waken to, and to our work and pleasure.
Though the body grows old and bears
the ache and weight of many days,
the life by which it lives is young,
for life is young or it does not
exist, is not even dead. And so
as I walk in the land's holy Sabbath
under the tall trees, I come
at once into the old young joy
that has moved me all my life to be
here in the early morning light.
But that is a dependent joy, granted
to me thrice seventeen years
by the other joy with which I return
in evening light to you, with old
love young through many sleeps.

VII

Having written some pages in favor of Jesus,
I receive a solemn communication crediting me
with the possession of a "theology" by which
I acquire the strange dignity of being wrong
forever or forever right. Have I gauged exactly
enough the weights of sins? Have I found
too much of the Hereafter in the Here? Or
the other way around? Have I found too much
pleasure, too much beauty and goodness, in this
our unreturning world? O Lord, please forgive
any smidgen of such distinctions I may
have still in my mind. I meant to leave them
all behind a long time ago. If I'm a theologian
I am one to the extent I have learned to duck
when the small, haughty doctrines fly overhead,
dropping their loads of whitewash at random
on the faces of those who look toward Heaven.
Look down, look down, and save your soul
by honester dirt, that receives with a lordly
indifference this off-fall of the air. Christmas
night and Easter morning are this soil's only laws.
The depth and volume of the waters of baptism,
the true taxonomy of sins, the field marks
of those most surely saved, God's own only
interpretation of the Scripture: these would be
causes of eternal amusement, could we forget
how we have hated one another, how vilified
and hurt and killed one another, bloodying
the world, by means of such questions, wrongly
asked, never to be rightly answered, but asked and
wrongly answered, hour after hour, day after day,
year after year—such is my belief—in Hell.

VIII

Hell is timely, for Hell is the thought
that Hell will go on, on and on, without end.
Heaven is only present, instantaneous and eternal,
a mayfly, a blue dayflower, a life entirely given,
complete forever in its hour.

IX

As if suddenly, little towns
where people once lived all
their lives in the same houses
now fill with strangers who
don't bother to speak or wave.
Life is a lonely business.
Gloss it how you will,
plaster it over with politic
bullshit as you please,
ours has been a brutal
history, punishing without
regret whatever or whomever
belonged or threatened to belong
in place, converting the land
to poverty and money any
way that was quickest. Now
after the long invasion
of alien species, including
our own, in a time of endangered
species, including our own,
we face the hard way: no choice
but to do better. After
the brief cataclysm of "cheap"
oil and coal has long
passed, along with the global
economy, the global village,
the hoards who go everywhere
and live nowhere, after
the long relearning, the long
suffering, the homecoming
that must follow, maybe
there will be a New World
of native communities again:
plants, animals, humans,

soils, stones, stories,
songs, all belonging
to such small, once known
and forgotten, officially unknown
and exploited, beautiful places
such as this, where despite
all we have done wrong
the golden light of October
falls through the turning leaves.
The leaves die and fall,
making wealth in the ground,
making in the ground the only
real material wealth.
Ignoring our paltry dream
of omniscience merely human,
the knowing old land
has lighted the woodland's edges
with the last flowers of the year,
the tiny asters once known
here as farewell-summer.

X

So many times I've gone away
from here, where I'd rather be
than any place I know, to go
off into the air for which
my only gift is breath, for I have
of myself no wings. It is death.
Farewell, my dearest ones.
Farewell, my lovely fields. Farewell,
my grazing flock, my patient horses,
Maggie my ardent dog. Farewell,
tall woods clarified by song.

However long I've stayed away,
coming home is resurrection. The man
who has been gone comes back to his place
as he would come naked and cold
into his own clothes. And they
are here, the known beloved: family,
neighbors obliging and dear. The dead,
too, denying their graves, haunt
the places they were known in and knew,
field and barn, riverbank and woods.
The familiar animals all are here.

Coming back is brightening in a grave,
such is the presage of old hymns.
To the place we parted from in sorrow
we return in joy: the beautiful shore,
eternal morning, unclouded day.

XI

Though he was ill and in pain,
in disobedience to the instruction he
would have received if he had asked,
the old man got up from his bed,
dressed, and went to the barn.
The bare branches of winter had emerged
through the last leaf-colors of fall,
the loveliest of all, browns and yellows
delicate and nameless in the gray light
and the sifting rain. He put feed
in the troughs for eighteen ewe lambs,
sent the dog for them, and she
brought them. They came eager
to their feed, and he who felt
their hunger was by their feeding
eased. From no place in the time
of present places, within no boundary
nameable in human thought,
they had gathered once again,
the shepherd, his sheep, and his dog
with all the known and the unknown
round about to the heavens' limit.
Was this stubbornness or bravado?
No. Only an ordinary act
of profoundest intimacy in a day
that might have been better. Still
the world persisted in its beauty,
he in his gratitude for which
he had most earnestly prayed.

XII

My people are destroyed for lack of knowledge . . .
Hosea 4:6

We forget the land we stand on
and live from. We set ourselves
free in an economy founded
on nothing, on greed verified
by fantasy, on which we entirely
depend. We depend on fire
that consumes the world without
lighting it. To this dark blaze
driving the inert metal
of our most high desire
we offer our land as fuel,
thus offering ourselves at last
to be burned. This is our riddle
to which the answer is a life
that none of us has lived.

XIII

By its own logic, greed
finally destroys itself,
as Lear's wicked daughters
learned to their horror, as
we are learning to our own.
What greed builds is built
by destruction of the materials
and lives of which it is built.
Only mourners survive.
This is the "creative destruction"
of which learnèd economists
speak in praise. But what is made
by destruction comes down at last
to a stable floor, a bed
of straw, and for those with sight
light in darkness.

I

For Giannozzo Pucci

"Why seek ye the living among the dead?"

Early in the year by my friend's gift
I saw at Sansepolcro Piero's vision:
The soldiers who guard the dead from the living
themselves become as dead men, one
tumbling dazedly backward. Awake, his wounds
bleeding still, his foot upon the tomb, Christ
who bore our life to its most wretched end,
having thrust off like a blanket the heavy lid,
stands. But for his face and countenance
I have found no words: powerful beyond life
and death, seeing beyond sight or light,
beyond all triumph serene. All this Piero saw.
And we who were sleeping, seeking the dead
among the dead, dare to be awake. We who see
see we are forever seen, by sight have been
forever changed. The morning at last
has come. The trees, once bare, are green.

II

We've come again to a garden begun,
to warmth after cold, and the spring sun
after long nights. And now, today,
we remember your birth and the way
you've come from then until now,
most of the way with me. Our old vow
has kept us returning again and again
to this garden that once more we begin,
that in our ways we both were born to,
work of love the passing sun cannot undo.

III

After windstorm and ice storm
the woods floor is a maze
of trunks and branches, heavy
bodies brought violently down,
and this is the fate they stood for.
In April now, after the cold
and the blows, rising in the tangle
so mightily shaken, broken, and fallen,
in their turn come the small flowers,
rue anemone and bluebell,
violet and larkspur. In these,
standing also in time to fall,
shines the world's great tenderness,
light and sight passingly touching
like a kiss. Made no doubt by force,
the world is saved by tenderness.
After they fall, the fallen decay
quietly, by countless gentle acts.

IV

How little I know in my widest
waking, held here by the making
of days, days of work, days,
fewer, of rest, suffering myself
to be made by days that cannot
be helped or changed or stopped,
and so I wait to be changed
by work, by rest, by what
I know into what I know not.

V

Tiny elegant birds, a pair, have come
again to nest in the chinquapin oak.
They are blue-gray gnatcatchers, or so
we call them. What they call themselves
we don't, will never, know
nor what they have in mind. To some
"objective" human minds, they are
small machines at the beck and call
of instinct, genetical—an insult
to them and to us all. Like humans,
creatures even so slight can live
only by thought. Like the syntax
of human speech, their nest survives
as a formal archetype, generation
after generation. They are born into it.
But to gather it into substantial being,
to build it actually in the place
afforded by the tree and chosen
by them—a place, a choice like no others—
they must think, as to speak
in the order of speech we were born into
the right sentence in the right place
at the right time—a place, a time
like no others—we too must think.
Let us praise, then, the least birds
who survive, after their kind, by thinking.

VI

Our vow is the plumb line,
the signature and sign
saying we are two, two
plighted to one life, the line
dividing us to let us speak,
to let us keep while we live
our promise to each other
in our need, openly to all
who care to see, but vanishing
as only we two know
when we indeed are one.

VII

For the apparent disorder
of the broken woods there are
reasons enough, although
we do not know them all
or their pattern, but by reasons
is disorder ordered, and so
we trust and live and love
this place whose belongings we are.
The woodland has no creed
except for the presumptive fact
that the pattern of its breaking
involves also, given time,
the pattern of its healing.

VIII

As old men often have said,
I don't know what this world
is coming to. I know at least
it is coming to the end
of cheap energy and cheap food
as it has come already to the end
of unpolluted water and air,
which makes this a good time to write
a poem about working with horses,
doing thus less damage to the world,
our fellow creatures, and ourselves.
Always there have been penalties
for Luddites, and I am one
familiar with the penalties,
though so far I have not been hanged.
Luddites are guilty of disrespect
to any silliness that is popular,
to any meanness that is profitable.
But I will say for the horses
that they live and move by sunlight,
they work at body temperature,
and are innocent of the fires
that are burning up the world.
They are innocent of the human powers
of explosion and poison. They are quiet.
They leave no blight. They do not
displace human work, but lighten it
and make it less lonely, unlike
the fire-driven machines that make
for themselves a secondary world.
And so I teach two grandchildren
to mow a field, using a team
of horses and a ground-driven mower
bought new sometime in the middle

of the last century, in my boyhood,
by my father or my grandfather.
To these new people growing up
in a world gravely diminished
between my childhood and theirs,
I say that this work requires them
to pay attention to many things:
to the team, the mower, the standing
grass and the fallen, to the place
of our work and the creatures who share it
between the bedrock and the sky,
for it is a living place of many
lives, complexly domestic.
I tell them our work, for good or ill,
is work of membership.
We know the worth of it by how
it looks and how it feels,
as we know by sympathy how
the horses stand the work. I tell them
that to work well they finally
must know without knowing
and think without thinking,
as a skilled musician touches
without forethought the right
string or key, so that the work
and all its parts are made one,
one motion of body and mind.
To please me at first, and then
to please themselves, the young ones
drive the long rounds of the pasture
in the ancient collaboration
of humans and horses, short time
gathering the sense of long time,
the day bright, the horses stepping
briskly to lift the heart, the cut
stems falling backward over

the blade. And this slow, lowly, artful,
necessary work receives
the validation of beauty. The work, itself
beautiful, is made more so
by swallows whose flight dips and winds
round and round the mower
as it sends insects flying upward
from the swath, by butterflies
everywhere that keep the air
alive, and by Emily and Marshall
as they learn anew a comely old way
nearly lost. Ghosts rejoice
in them in me as I rejoice.

IX

In Memory: James Baker Hall

The old know well the world
is the place of the absence of many
known, loved, and gone,
as the mind might contain a sky
empty of birds, an earth
without landmark trees.
The young, the husbands and wives,
must learn and the old recall
that all the absent are not gone.
Many are still to come.
The spring of grief also is
the spring of joy. The cup
is dipped and drunk, and the space
of its taking again is filled.

X

Our young Tanya, who bears
the fine name of her granny
into the years to come,
intelligent blue eyes
lighting the way—Oh, honey,
how we love you! How we
look after you, as time
passes and goes on.

As I speak to you I hear
in my voice the voice
of my own granny, the clear
candor of her love, still
speaking for us all.

XI

O Thou who by Thy touch give form
To all things and their polity,
Whose sight is light to all, draw thanks
From us as we draw breath from Thee.

XII

"Maybe," Mr. Ernest said. "The best word in our language, the best of all."
William Faulkner, "Race at Morning"

At the end of a long time
the book keeper sits down with his book.
He enters all that he has learned
of suffering, grief, and ugliness,
of cruelty, waste, and loss,
stupidity, meanness, falsehood,
selfishness, loneliness, and greed.
He reckons all these as a great
weight he has no way of weighing.
He enters then all he has learned
of joy, goodness, beauty, love,
of generosity, grace, and laughter,
good sense, honesty, compassion,
mercy, and forgiveness.
And these also weigh an unweighable
weight that registers only
on his heart. He cannot at last
complete and close his book.
He cannot say of evil and good
which outweighs the other,
though he feels his time's rage
for quantification, and he would like
to know. He only can suppose
the things of goodness, the most
momentary, are in themselves
so whole, so bright as to redeem
the darkness and trouble of the world
though we set it all afire.
"Maybe," the bookkeeper says. "Maybe."
For he knows that in a time
gone mad for certainty, "maybe"
gives room to live and move and be.

I

When icy fangs hang from the eaves,
And the arms shiver in their sleeves,
The world in beauty, white and stark,
Emerges light-forced from the dark.

The sheep wake buried in the new
Earth of the snow. They rise up, ewe
By ewe, and shake themselves, to pass
From sleep uphill to dig for grass
Through snow in falling snow all day.
The bare bed-places where they lay,
Their dark unmoving shadows on
The old earth, in a while are blown
White, disappear, and there's no sign
Of sheep before the hour they're in.

The speckled sparrow, the junco
Pick up dry grass seed from the snow.
They live by scatters that they find,
Survive by favor of the wind.

The field mouse made by hunger brave
Returns to light outside his cave,
His nest in grass stems and dry sticks,
To leave a dangerous script of tracks
Soon end-stopped by a dot of blood
—By need to eat transformed to food.

Cold closes round our house at night,
To open only when sunlight
Shows frost-flakes shining in the air.
We live by stored food and by fire,
By knowing how we've lived before,
By faith that spring will come once more.

Snow crossed our fences undenied,
And modern ease is nullified.
Like mice and sparrows, so to speak,
We're squeaking by. We hear the squeak.

II

Many with whom I mourned the dead
Are dead, and mourn no more. Blessèd
Are they that mourn, for thus they have
The fullest magnitude of love
And learn of it, whereby the dead
Outlive their lives, and live instead
Eternally in present grace
Where death, ashamed, can find no place,
For love goes with them, out of time
Passing, and mercy welcomes them.
Lest in our grief we lose our way,
The dead lead back to light of day.
Not their absence from us we mourn,
But ours from them, and this we learn.

III

Where he sat in a room apart
from all he had ever known,
alone in Easter morning light,
I read him the story of Magdalene
grieving at the tomb alone,
and the appearing Gardener:
"Why weepest thou? Whom
seekest thou?" From far in absence,
in silence, he heard me. "That
is a beautiful story," he told me.

IV

Fifty-three years gone,
I prepared for our marriage here,
working day by bright day
beneath the green leaves
of May, the river flowing then
as time ever has flowed, has flown,
as day by day I made ready
our passing stay beside it.

✦

All it has so far been
is past, long past, and yet
I see it with the young eyes
of that May, present as today.

V

The red-eyed vireo
who bent the lithe branch
and fluttered the leaves,
returning to her eggs,
has disappeared. Her nest
will fill with snow.

VI

Let us not condemn the human beings
self-appointed to serve machines,
poor humans, so weak of mind,
so self-misled, so willing to risk
heroic wrong. What's the satisfaction in
condemning the self-condemned?
Let them be answered by themselves
who grow smaller, their great works
uglier, more lethal, day by day.
As we wish, ourselves, to be spared
the fatal numbering, let us not
confound offenders with offenses.
May they come to mercy and to peace.

But damn their bank accounts, inflated
by the spent breath of all the earth,
of species forever changed to money.
Let their legal falsehoods, corpses
incorporated that cannot see
or feel, think or care, that eat
the world and shit money, fry
in Hell in their own fat. May
their incarnate steel and fire
that destroy the mountains forever
be damned. May the chemicals
be damned that poison the rivers
and damned too the alien slop and fume
that spoil the air, the water, and all
the living world, sold, soiled, or burned.
May the plastic trash that defiles lands
and oceans, the machines that destroy
the work of human hands, the mind-
destroying mechanical dreams be damned,
completely damned. Be damned also

to the incorporations of industrial war
that is the triumph of every machine,
that will destroy any life and every life,
any place and every place, for victory
that always is defeat. May the heartless
speech of machines that break the heart
of the smallest wholeness, and may
the radiant waste that has made geniuses
idiots forever be damned.

It's poor religion that can't provide
a sufficient curse when needed, but
if you condemn the dire shortcuts
and devices of the engineers, confess
that you condemn yourself. You too
belong to that litter, and so must enter
your guilty plea, and so must come
to your work. You must go ahead
in opposition to the mechanical life,
continuing also the creaturely task, longer
than your life, of correcting yourself.

VII

Blesséd be the vireo
who, leaving, leaves
not even a track.

VIII

If you love it, do not photograph
the woods as it now is, the leaves
in sunlight and shadow hardly stirring
in the air of the hot afternoon.
Do not try to remember it, stopping
the flutters of leaves and wings,
the dead leaf slowly spinning
on an invisible thread. Do not ask
the trees to linger even to be named.
You must live in the day as it passes,
willing to let it go. You must set it
free. You must forget this poem.
Then, into its own time forever
gone, it is forever here.

IX

By courtesy of the light
we have the beautiful shadows.
Because the trees darken
the ground, shade-lovers thrive.
To one who stands outside,
the woods is a wall of leaves
impassable by sight, passable
by foot or wing. Come in
and walk among the shades.

X

Anger at humans, my own kind—
I remember how it carried me,
joyous in self's self-exaltation,
through a narrow opening as at birth
into the great hollow of the dark itself
where the unappeasable, in unending
revenge for revenge, tread each
alone the circle of no known
beginning or end. And that is Hell.

XI

The need comes on me now
to speak across the years
to those who finally will live here
after the present ruin, in the absence
of most of my kind who by now
are dead, or have given their minds
to machines and become strange,
"over-qualified" for the hard
handwork that must be done
to remake, so far as humans
can remake, all that humans
have unmade. To you, whoever
you may be, I say: Come,
meaning to stay. Come,
willing to learn what this place,
like no other, will ask of you
and your children, if you mean
to stay. "This land responds
to good treatment," I heard
my father say time and again
in his passion to renew, to make
whole, what ill use had broken.
And so to you, whose lives
taken from the life of this place
I cannot foretell, I say:
Come, and treat it well.

XII

To those who love one another
the thought of Heaven is native
as the thought of food. We dream
our need: the beautiful shore
where loved ones will greet us
in the unclouded day. My father,
old, named over the dear ones
he had outlived: "If they are there,
Heaven is Paradise indeed."

XIII

O my own small country, battered
wife of my kind, made in time
by life and its multiple ends,
dying and rising again,
you come to mere use, which is
misuse by life self-estranged.
Life is not of the body,
For death disembodies it,
and yet it suffers. Only life
suffers, as you suffer
use without care or thanks.
They who abuse you live
by your life, they thrive
a while by your ruin.
But now let us think instead
of a husband and a wife, one
flesh, whose flesh is one
with their place, grace
unearned, your gift, by which
they are made your own.

I

For David Garrard Lowe

Matisse's Dominique of Vence*
on a postcard from a friend
stands in my window, a presence
in the light, below a bend

of the Kentucky River.
His face is featureless,
yet he stands in character,
a book displaying a cross

held against his heart
by a hand in bare outline,
remade entirely by art.
The falling folds of his gown

are several vertical strokes
signifying to the eye
in black lines quick as looks.
The saint is standing by

in silence while the light
performs its holy work
in colors on the white
wall. After the dark

it is morning in Vence.
Many years ago
I went there, and ever since
have recalled the light, now

replaced by later light,
how it filled the room,
crowding the darkness out,
allowing vision its time.

Behind the pictured saint,
meanwhile, my washed window
is a grid in black paint
rationally ruled, although

admitting sensational light. Beyond
are trees, the river, a dark line of hills,
familiar as hand to mind,
but the prospect fills

no term of human truth,
no form of human thought.
A heron hunched at stream mouth
fishes quietly as he ought.

*A figure in outline of St. Dominique, one of Matisse's "decorations" for the
Chapel of the Rosary in Vence, a hill town in southern France. The Chapel
was consecrated on June 25, 1951. I went there in 1962.

II

Moonlight, daylight,
pink clouds eastward,
cries of geese flying
north, the river quiet.
Heavenly the bluebells
whose freshness cannot
be remembered from one
April until the next.

III

Quiet. The river flows soundlessly by
at the speed of its own long time.
The pregnant ewes, the ewes with new lambs
are safe in the barn for the night, fed,
feeding, and quiet. Here in the shadow
of the westward hill, I see
through the budding trees the green
sunlit fields, the sunlit leafless woods,
quiet, on the far side of the river.
The stillness remains, not a plane in the air,
not a car on the road. How rare this brief
peace. The machines of death draw
breath from the sky. Give thanks to the quiet.

IV

At the woods' edge, suddenly
the air around him was perfumed
with the scent of wild plum flowers.
The whitened trees were accompanied
by several redbuds also in bloom,
equally beautiful, and both
together more beautiful than either
alone. Nothing in the long winter
prepared him to imagine this, a moment
in a thousand years never old.

V

For years around the spare house
beside the river, his clear room
of quiet, he preserved an opening,
a lawn half-kept that signified
outside his inside occupation,
half keeping what he more than half
had lost. Later, he withdrew his blades.
Slowly the house in its clearing
has become a house in the woods.
Saplings and seedlings of sugar maple,
hickory, hackberry, walnut, ash,
box elder, chinquapin, wild cherry,
rough-leaf dogwood, spice bush,
elderberry have come to renew
around it their old companionship.
Under them, over their dead leaves,
spring woodsflowers come to light,
and this year at last a fern.
Within a radius all around,
he has uprooted the garlic mustard,
an exotic invader of the native woods.
Only semi-native himself, he thinks
of all the miles he has traveled
to talk of conservation, his wayfare
poisoning the air, burning the earth,
contradicting this place, where
he joins the living world.

VI

The old shepherd comes to another
lambing time, and he gives thanks.
He has longed ever more strongly
as the weeks and months went by
for the new lives the ewes have carried
in their bellies through the winter cold.
Now in gray early mornings of barely
spring he goes to see at last
what the night has revealed.

Through many of its generations
he has husbanded his flock, keeping
every year a few promising ewe lambs
to replace the old that die and those
that fail, are culled, and sold. Some
of any year's crop will be better
than the rest, some will be outstanding.
The best he remembers from the time,
as sucklings, they caught his eye.

Lineages of motherhood having stayed
unbroken through many years,
his flock has improved, somewhat by
his choosing, no doubt, but more
as the farm itself has chosen them
for their thriving in it, on its
terms, and so they are its own.
They belong by adapting to the place
as the shepherd wishes to belong.

VII

A man who loves the trees
walks among them on a dark day
for the solace he has taken always
from the company of his elders,
and suddenly he sees
such a grace as in all his going
he is always going toward
though never in his foreknowing:
among duller trunks and branches
a dogwood flower-white
lighting all the woods.

April 30, 2011

VIII

Off in the woods in the quiet
morning a redbird is singing
and his song goes out around him
greater than its purpose,
a welcoming room of song
in which the trees stand,
through which the creek flows.

IX

I have watched this place,
fearing for it in the storms
of history, three score years
and ten and more. What,
then, after so long awake,
do I affirm? Human-hurt
as it is, it is unending
in its beauty, hour by hour.

X

I saw a hummingbird stand
in midair and scratch his cheek
vigorously with his left foot,
as he might have done perched
at ease upon a tree. "Wonderful!"
I said to myself. "I never dreamed
of such a thing before, and now
after seventy-seven years
of watching, I have seen it!"

XI

New come, we took fields
from the forest, clearing, breaking
the steep slopes. And this was
a fall from a kind of grace:
from the forest in its long Sabbath,
dependent only upon
the Genius of this place, to the field
dependent upon us, our work,
and our failure first and last
to keep peace between
the naked soil and the rain.
From the laws of the First Former
we fell to the place deformed.
The hard rains fell then
into our history, from grace
to fate upon our gullied land.

We numbered the years, not many,
until the forest took back
the failed fields with their scars
unhealed and long in healing,
our toil forfeit to the trees
of a new generation: locust,
cedar, box elder, elm,
and thorn. In spring the redbud
and wild plum, white and pink
on the abandoned slopes, granted
such beauty as we might
have thought forgiving.

By leaving it alone, we are
in a manner forgiven. And yet
we must wait long, long—
how much longer than we

will live?—for the return of what
is gone, not of the past
forever lost, but of health,
the promise of life in land
remade finally whole.

Left alone, the "pioneer
generation" of trees gives way
to the oaks, hickories, maples,
beeches, poplars of the lasting
forest.

　　　　By keeping intact
its gift of self-renewal, not
as our belonging, but asking how
we might belong to it,
what we might use of it
for ourselves, leaving it whole,
we may come to live in its
time, in which our lives will pass
as pass the lives of birds
within the lives of trees.

XII

Do not live for death,
pay it no fear or wonder.
This is the firmest law
of the truest faith. Death
is the dew that wets the grass
in the early morning dark.
It is God's entirely. Withdraw
your fatal homage, and live.

XIII

Will-lessly the leaves fall,
are blown, coming at last
to the ground and to their rest.
Among them in their coming down
purposely the birds pass,
of all the unnumbered ways
choosing one, until
they like the leaves will
will-lessly fall. Thus freed
by gravity, every one
enters the soil, conformed
to the craft and wisdom, the behest
of God's appointed vicar,
our mother and judge, who binds
us each to each, the largest
to the least, in the family of all
the creatures: great Nature
by whom all are changed, none
are wasted, none are lost.
Supreme artist of this
our present world, her works
live and move, love
their places and their lives in them.
And this is praise to the highest
knowledge by the most low.

I

Now falls upon our hope and work
The year's end and the early dark.

The river on its ceaseless flow all day
Bears widening circles of the rain away.

II

Like light beyond "the visible spectrum,"
prayer goes up from the nursing home
from this detritus, these cast aside.
Ones I loved who committed the wrong,
the great estrangement, of living
too long, they too sent up from this
foreign land, their exile, the vast
supplication of extreme humanity:
Help me. Help us. Help the dying
to die. Help the dead to live. Maybe
they have dwindled to final care, to
final prayer. Maybe they have come
to the final freedom, no longer wanting
time, no longer wanting. From the farms
and the little towns they have been
gathered unto this last. Low down
as its source may be, their prayer
ascends, it rises as out of the grave,
it is a glory of the earth. If this is not
true, what do I know that is?

III

Though his tenure on the earth
is that of a blade of grass,
though his acquaintance among the dead
increases year by year
and, like many grown old
before, he lives from the loss
of one beloved companion
to the loss of yet another,
the old man prays to find,
at the end of his own leash,
his love for the world at hand,
his heart at rest in gratitude.

Still, his old nightmares
return. He dreams of permanent
destruction, his country broken,
its woodlands felled, its streams
poisoned. The future devilne,
in his mind, his life shattered
and strewn in the public way,
his dreams recall the night
of Gethsemane, the fear
that the end of the way taken
is not to die merely,
but to die forsaken, the heart
finally broken.

                    From this
despair he asks to be
remade, set free, let go
if only into the sanity of grief,
if only to suffer the suffering

of old companions he has loved
and loves. Sometimes his love
returns, finds him in his dream,
and leads him home.

IV

It's spring. The birds sing.
And how explain their singing?
The objective biologist wishes
to know. He knows! Sex.
The genes' imperative to survive
in a hostile world. His bird
is the Poppy Cock. The birds
of the actual woodland sing
to the season and their dearest loves
their beautiful offering,
as long ago Chaucer
knew, who knew also
that all love songs come
from the one Muse: "Blessed
be Seynt Valentyn,
For on this day I chees yow
to be myn, Withouten
repentyng myn herte swpetp!"
So sang the "smale fowles"
in the time-delighted trees
in Chaucer's hearing and in ours
eternal mystery.

V

The grass doth wither, the flower
doth fade. I fear to dispute
the Prophets, but it is ungrateful
to complain, accounting
brevity as a fault. The glory
of God, I grant although
I do not "know," goes on
forever, but the lowliest
flowers blooming now
—beautiful in the spring woods
among garlic mustard,
other foreign competitors,
and the forever alien industrial
humans—the fleetingest blossoms
of twinleaf and bloodroot also
glorify God and are
eternal in their moment.

VI

"Attend to the little ones,"
said William Blake, and long
before Blake spoke or wrote
shepherds obeyed him, watching
over the births of lambs.
Like human beings at the beginning
and the end of their lives, these
little ones are in need
of everything, having not
a breath that is not given.
By Nature's gift they live,
and at times by human help,
the shepherd finding in himself
the world's tenderness deeply
planted, sorrow always
that even the least should be lost.

VII

Under the sign of the citizen's pistol,
under the sign of the corporate dozer,
we meet again: the modest flowers
of the woods, faithful to this place
where they have belonged a few days
every spring for years uncountable,
and I, who have known them only
for most of the years of a human life.
Though I am worn with the years
I have awaited them, they arrive
each spring young as before.
Where the native membership
remains intact, the flowers cover
the ground, in surplus of perfection,
quietly radiant, unexplained.
So much given, so few who know.
So much beauty, so little love.

VIII

Since, despite the stern demands
of scientist and realist, we will always
be supposing, let us suppose
that Nature gave the world flowers
and birdsong as a language, by which
it might speak to discerning humans.
And what must we say back? Not
just thanks or praise, but acts
of kindness bespeaking kinship
with the creatures and with Nature, acts
faithful as the woods that dwells in place
time out of mind, self-denying
as the parenthood of the birds, and like
the flowers humble and beautiful.

IX

I rest in the one life
of husband and wife.
Convergence of two alone
amounts to one,
the most lowly sum,
which can't be fallen from
but into fraction,
the direst subtraction.
When we two are wholly gone
and are at one
we are in place,
without a trace
from our selves departed
and single hearted.

5/29/12

X

In memory: Ivan Illich

The creek flows full over the rocks
after lightning, thunder, and heavy rain.
Its constant old song rises under
the still unblemished green, new leaves
of old sycamores that have so far
withstood the hardest flows. And this
is the flux, the thrust, the slow song
of the great making, the world never
at rest, still being made
of the ever less and less that we,
for the time being, make of it.

XI

There are seasons enough for sorrow
but best be sorrowful in spring
when the martins at last return
to their houses near the porch,
the barn swallows to the barn.
You can't be entirely sorrowful,
watching the swallows flying
to live, and ever delighted
to be flying. They know perfectly
that they are beautiful. And the good
never is made less good
by subtracting badness from it.

XII

Once there was nothing,
not even darkness,
not even silence,
not even nothing.
Think of that.

XIII

The eastern sky at evening
curves down from blue to white
to hilltops across the river.
Nearer, a few treetops
are sunbright among the trees
in shadow. The moment is clear
as water, still as stone.
As it is, nobody could paint it,
nor I describe or remember it.
A photograph might keep
its lights and shades, its colors
maybe, but not the air,
the breath by which it lives,
visible only fleetly
in the eyes' living light,
and in an eyewink changed.
Surely its quickly passing
perfects forever its beauty.
And so again the mortal
has fallen short of the real.

XIV

Praise "family values,"
"a better future for our children,"
displacing meanwhile the familiar
membership to be a "labor force"
of homeless strangers. Praise
work and name it "jobs."
With "labor-saving technology"
replace workers at their work
and hold them in contempt
because they have no "jobs."
Praise "our country" and oppress
the land with poisons, gouges,
blastings, the violent labors and
pleasures of the unresting displaced,
skinning the earth alive.
This is the way, the truth, and the life.

Welcome the refugees set free
from the "nowhere" of rural America,
from the "drudgery" of the household
and the "mind-numbing work"
of shops and farms, into
the anthills of "liberation,"
the endless vistas of "growth,"
of "progress," the "limitless adventure
of the human spirit" rising
through inward emptiness into
"outer space." Welcome
the displaced naturally "upwardly
mobile" to their "better world"
as they gather bright-lighted
in "multicultural" masses
in the packed streets. Catch
those who inevitably

fall from the light-swarm
in meshes of "safety nets," "benefits,"
"job training," the army,
the wars, mental hospitals,
jails, graves. Forget
vocation, memory, living
and dying at home. This
is the way, the truth, and the life.

Flourish your weapons of official
war where they are needed
for peace, bring death by chance
but needfully to small houses
where children play at war
or a wedding is taking place
so that the bride and the groom
will not be separately killed,
for you have an enemy
somewhere, who must be killed.
Therefore forgive the unofficial
entrepreneur who brings
your weapons to your
school, your office, your
neighborhood theater, bringing
death randomly but needfully,
for his enemies are his
as yours are yours. This is
the way, the truth, and the life.

XV

On a bright day, having slept
a long nap in the woods,
he woke out of sleep's darkness
to find the sky come low
to the tops of the tallest trees.
Between the sky and the earth
lights and shadows darted
and danced among the leaves.

XVI

There is no spring flower so
brilliant and bright as the red
spice bush berries
ripe in the fall, lighting
as the sun strikes them among
the still green leaves,
and no structure so beautiful
before the killing frost
as the brown spider's radial
web, connecting all points
of the lived life, shining
with the caught morning light
across my path, and so
I see it in time, and walk
around it through tall weeds
to leave it undisturbed.

XVII

After the long weeks
when the heat curled the leaves
and the air thirsted, comes
a morning after rain, cool
and bright. The leaves uncurl,
the pastures begin again
to grow, the animals and the birds
rejoice. If tonight the world
ends, we'll have had this day.

XVIII

This is the flood road,
the broken way the water
passes when the sky bursts
and hell breaks loose
in this crease at the hills' feet
as the rain gathers and plunges
in its never-ending search
for the world's floor. And here
by night the spider weaves
her fragile work by touch
in the dark to shine by day.

XIX

This is the age of our absence from the world, even
while we are living in it. We now are ghosts,
disembodied of original soil by our mortal hurts
to earth, water, air, and light. The native
willow trees, our old neighbors, are gone
from the river, and who has noticed?
Poisons drain from mines and fields, are secreted
in the water, and who has come to drink?
The dominion of anonymity clouds over the land
where voices of machines guide us through the dark.
Our people, neighbors once, have left homes and names
to stray in the public ways, loose money
spent at the bidding of machines. At the Crucifixion
they stand and watch, having bartered their flesh
as the price of admission. They believe this death
is a show, and they duly consent to be diverted.
In their public language they can say nothing true.
In that speech whatever is said that is true
is a lie. Under the public cloud blighted
humans swarm like flies upon a wound.

XX

Sit and be quiet. In a while
the red berries, now in shadow,
will be picked out by the sun.

XXI

As a child, the Mad Farmer saw easily
the vision of Heaven's Christ born in a stable,
the brilliant star stopped in the high dark,
the sheltered beasts standing silently by.
He knows the beasts, he is himself a shepherd,
and still, more clearly, by the gift of a moment,
he sees the shepherds on their cold hill by night,
the sky flying suddenly open over their heads,
the light of very Heaven falling upon them,
the angels descending, slowly as snow, their singing
filling far and wide the dark: "On earth
peace, good will." The vision, the gift
only of moments, he has kept in his eyes, in his heart.
He knows how it passes, how it fades,
how it stays, how far we have drawn away.
He thinks of distance, the hard hungry journey
of a foolish man, a pilgrim in the foreshadow
of apocalypse, toward the almost forgotten
light far beyond the polluted river,
the blasted mountains, the killed children, the bombed
villages haunted already by the hurting bodies
of their dead. Some of the past he dreads as if
it has not yet happened. From present portent
he fears the time to come. Beyond and beyond
is the shepherd-startling, ever-staying light.
No creature of his slow-minded kind may ever
stand in that light again. He sets out.

Index of First Lines

A bird the size   170

A child unborn, the coming year   39

A gracious lady came to us   256

A gracious Sabbath stood here while
   they stood   64

A hawk in flight   281

A long time ago, returning   168

A man is lying on a bed   153

A man is walking in a field   318

A man who loves the trees   366

A man with some authentic
   worries   157

A man's desire, overwhelming   316

A mind that has confronted ruin for
   years   220

A tired man leaves his labor, felt   56

A young man leaving home   249

After a mild winter   224

After the bitter nights   315

After the campaign of the killing
   machines   246

After the long weeks   393

After the slavery of the body,
   dumbfoundment   100

After windstorm and ice storm   331

Again I resume the long   201

Again we come   131

All that patriotism requires, and all
   that it can be   245

All yesterday afternoon I sat   234

Alone, afoot, in moonless night   210

Always in the distance   85

An old man, who has been on many
   days   259

And now the lowland grove is down,
   the trees   77

And now the remnant groves grow
   bright with praise   79

And now this leaf lies brightly on the
   ground   155

Anger at humans, my own kind   354

Another Sunday morning comes   8

Another year has returned us   83

"Are you back to normal?" asks   263

As a child, the Mad Farmer saw
   easily   397

As if suddenly, little towns   323

As old men often have said   336

As timely as a river   207

Ask the world to reveal its
   quietude   219

At the end of a long time   342

At the woods' edge, suddenly   363

"Attend to the little ones"   381

Awaked from the persistent dream   65

Before we kill another child   294

Best of any song   173

Blesséd be the vireo   351

Born by our birth   282

But do the Lords of War in fact   247

By courtesy of the light   353

By expenditure of hope   188

By its own logic, greed   328

Camp Branch, my native
   stream [The Book of Camp
   Branch]   285

Can I see the buds that are
   swelling   195

398

Come to the window, look out, and
   see [Look Out]   239
Coming to the woods' edge   73
Cut off in front of the line   104
Do not live for death   372
Dream ended, I went out, awake   35
Early in the morning, walking   185
Early in the year by my friend's
   gift   329
Enclosing the field within
   bounds   19
Estranged by distance, he
   relearns   61
Eternity is not infinity   274
Even while I dreamed I prayed that
   what I saw was only fear and no
   foretelling   174
Every afternoon the old turtle   233
Fifty-three years gone   347
Finally will it not be enough   149
For the apparent disorder   335
For the third time since the first [The
   Locusts]   320
For years around the spare
   house   364
Given the solemn river   191
Go by the narrow road [The
   Farm]   114
God, how I hate the names   275
Great deathly powers have
   passed   27
Hail to the forest born again   46
Hardly escaping the limitless
   machines   280
Hate has no world   144
Having written some pages in favor
   of Jesus   321
He had a tall cedar he wanted to cut

for posts [The Old Man Climbs
   a Tree]   163
He thought to keep himself from
   Hell   92
He wakes in darkness. All
   around   217
Hell is timely, for Hell is the
   thought   322
Here by the road where people are
   carried, with   94
Here in the woods near   269
Here where the dark-sourced stream
   brims up   36
Here where the world is being
   made   33
How can we be so superior   295
How little I know in my widest   332
How long does it take to make the
   woods   67
How many have relinquished   14
How many of your birthdays   319
How simple to be dead! — the
   only   266
I am hardly an ornithologist   277
I built a timely room beside the
   river   254
I climb up through the thicket   75
I dream by night the horror   297
I dream of a quiet man   196
I go among trees and sit still   7
I go by a field where once   309
I go from the woods into the cleared
   field   18
I have again come home   136
I have watched this place   368
I know for a while again   209
I know I am getting old and I
   say so   267

I know that I have life   261
I leave the warmth of the stove   147
I love the passing light   310
I mistook your white head for a
   flower   258
I rest in the one life   384
I saw a hummingbird stand   369
I think of Gloucester, blind, led
   through the world   150
I too am not at home   133
I tremble with gratitude   268
I walk in openings   101
I walked the deserted prospect of
   the modern mind [Santa Clara
   Valley]   89
I was wakened from my dream of the
   ruined world by the sound   176
I went away only   132
I would not have been a poet   154
I've come down from the sky   213
If there are a "chosen few"   283
If we have become a people
   incapable   273
If you love it, do not
   photograph   352
In a crease of the hill   49
In a single motion the river comes
   and goes   187
In early morning we awaken
   from   87
In Heaven the starry saints will wipe
   away   199
In our consciousness of time   302
In spring we planted seed   171
In the world forever one   205
In time a man disappears   307
Inside its bends, the river   317
Is this the river of life   229

It is almost spring again   167
It is hard to have hope. It is harder as
   you grow old   305
It is late November,
   Thanksgiving   248
It is the destruction of the world   82
It takes all time to show
   eternity   257
It's spring. The birds sing   379
Late winter cold   223
Learn by little the desire for all
   things   312
Let us not condemn the human
   beings   349
Life forgives its depredations   68
Lift up the dead leaves   130
Like light beyond "the visible
   spectrum"   376
Little stream, Camp Branch,
   flowing   291
Loving you has taught me the
   infinite   127
Many I loved as man and boy [Old
   Man Jayber Crow]   284
Many with whom I mourned the
   dead   345
Matisse's Dominique of Vence   359
May what I've written here   78
Moonlight, daylight   361
Mowing the hillside pasture—
   where   270
My sore ran in the night   134
My young grandson rides with
   me   272
Nell's small grave, opening   265
New come, we took fields   370
No, no, there is no going back   141
Not again in this flesh will I see   63

Now falls upon our hope and
    work   375
Now I have reached the age   81
Now Loyce Flood is dead   91
Now though the season warms   52
Now with its thunder spring   108
Now you have slipped away   165
Now you know the worst   162
Now, as a man learning   179
Now, surely, I am getting old   143
O my own small country,
    battered   357
O saints, if I am even eligible for this
    prayer   292
O Thou who by Thy touch give
    form   341
Off in the woods in the quiet   367
On a bright day, having slept   391
On summer evenings we sat in the
    yard   166
Once there was nothing,   387
One day I walked imagining   96
One morning out of time   93
Our Christmas tree is   172
Our household for the time made
    right   45
Our vow is the plumb line   334
Our young Tanya, who bears   340
Over the river in loud flood   55
Poem, do not raise your voice   308
Praise "family values"   389
Quiet. The river flows soundlessly
    by   362
Raking hay on a rough slope   152
Remembering that it happened
    once   80
Seventeen more years, and they are
    here [The Locusts]   111

Since, despite the stern
    demands   383
Sit and be quiet. In a while   396
Six days of work are spent   29
Slowly, slowly, they return   71
So many times I've gone away   325
Some had derided him   211
Some Sunday afternoon, it may
    be   169
Surely it will be for this: the
    redbud   218
Tanya. Now that I am getting
    old   193
"That's been an oak tree a long
    time"   296
Teach me work that honors Thy
    work   235
The Acadian flycatcher, not   227
The bell calls in the town   11
The best reward in going to the
    woods   158
The body in the invisible   103
The cherries turn ripe, ripe   228
The clearing rests in song and
    shade   44
The creek flows full over the
    rocks   385
The crop must drink; we move the
    pipe   59
The dark around us, come   47
The difference is a polished   202
The eager dog lies strange and
    still   26
The eastern sky at evening   388
The ewes crowd to the mangers   107
The flocking blackbirds fly
    across   232
The frog with lichened back and

golden thigh   28
The fume and shock and
    uproar   66
The grass doth wither, the
    flower   380
The house is cold at dawn   208
The incarnate Word is with us   203
The intellect so ravenous to
    know   30
The kindly faithful light
    returns   238
The little stream sings   241
The lovers know the loveliness   178
The nation is a boat   299
The need comes on me now   355
The old know well the world   339
The old oak wears new leaves   88
The old shepherd comes to
    another   365
The painter Harlan Hubbard
    said   276
"The past above, the future
    below   313
The pasture, bleached and cold two
    weeks ago   37
The politics of illusion, of death's
    money   242
The question before me, now
    that I   222
The red-eyed vireo   348
The seed is in the ground   110
The sky bright after summer-ending
    rain   95
The sounds of engines leave the
    air   311
The spring woods hastening
    now   197
The summer ends, and it is time   60

The team rests in shade at the
    edge   109
The times are disgusting
    enough   290
The two, man and boy, wait   97
The wind of the fall is here   221
The winter world of loss   129
The winter wren is back, quick   69
The woods and pastures are
    joyous   186
The woods is white with snow   237
The world of machines is
    running   84
The year begins with war   105
The year relents, and free   50
The yellow-throated warbler, the
    highest remotest voice   243
There are seasons enough for
    sorrow   386
There is a day   181
There is a place you can go   190
There is no spring flower so   392
They are fighting again the war to
    end war   252
They come singly, the little
    streams   251
They gather like an ancestry   262
They sit together on the porch, the
    dark   151
This is a poet of the river lands   3
This is the age of our absence from
    the world, even   395
This is the flood road   394
This is the time you'd like to
    stay   184
This, then, is to be the way?
    Freedom's candle will be   244
Those who give their thought   135

402

Those who use the world
    assuming   304
Though he was ill and in pain   326
Though his tenure on the
    earth   377
Thrush song, stream song, holy
    love   38
Times will come as they must   4
Tiny elegant birds, a pair, have
    come   333
To give mind to machines, they are
    calling it   99
To long for what can be fulfilled in
    time   21
To long for what eternity fulfills   23
To sit and look at light-filled
    leaves   10
To think of gathering all   253
To those who love one another   356
Under the sign of the citizen's
    pistol   382
Up in the blown-down woods   255
We come at last to the dark   226
We follow the dead to their
    graves   215
We forget the land we stand
    on   327
We have kept to the way we chose
    [Thirty-five Years]   138
We have walked so many times, my
    boy   40
We hear way off approaching
    sounds   212
We live by mercy if we live [Amish
    Economy]   160

We travelers, walking to the sun,
    can't see   200
We went in darkness where
    [Remembering Evia]   145
We were standing by the road   264
We've come again to a garden
    begun   330
What a consolation it is, after   198
What do the tall trees say   113
What hard travail God does in
    death   25
What I fear most is despair   192
What if, in the high, restful
    sanctuary   16
What stood will stand, though all be
    fallen   15
Whatever happens   183
Whatever is foreseen in joy   20
When icy fangs hang from the
    caves   343
When my father was an old
    man   142
When we convene again   206
Where he sat in a room apart   346
Where the great trees were
    felled   112
Who makes a clearing makes a work
    of art   53
Will-lessly the leaves fall   373
Worn to brightness, this [A Brass
    Bowl]   159
Yes, though hope is our duty   301
"You see," my mother said, and
    laughed   177

On the pages whose numbers are given below
the page end coincides with a stanza break:

8	115	249
11	119	270
12	121	277
16	122	278
21	145	287
30	179	297
56	188	313
57	193	343
73	229	359
101	230	